"Searing, heart-breaking, triumphant: *Brutal Legacy* is for anyone who's been punched in the face by someone they loved and then stood up again. It's for every mother who has run, and every sister who has picked up the pieces. This book is for every friend who hasn't fled, and for every co-worker who didn't know what to do; it's for every brother who's cried and for the children who have watched.

"In her beautiful book, Tracy Going reminds us that strength is hard won and courage lies with us all in glorious abundance once we find it. Every South African should read it."

– Sisonke Msimang, author of *Always Another Country*

Brutal Legacy
A memoir

Tracy Going

This book is based on my memory and events as I recall them; however, a few names have been changed to protect the privacy of the people involved.

First published by MFBooks Joburg, an imprint of
Jacana Media (Pty) Ltd, in 2018

10 Orange Street
Sunnyside
Auckland Park 2092
South Africa
+2711 628 3200
www.jacana.co.za

© Tracy Going, 2018

All rights reserved.

ISBN 978-1-928420-12-5

Cover design by publicide
Set in Sabon 11/15pt
Printed by Creda Communications
Job no. 003160

See a complete list of Jacana titles at www.jacana.co.za

*To Chase, Ashleigh and David,
for all the broken bits*

Prologue

"He murdered her."

"Who? Who murdered who?"

"Oscar. He murdered his girlfriend, Reeva Steenkamp," I repeat.

"What happened?" My husband is still half asleep.

I set my coffee cup aside, adjust my glasses and read the story out loud.

"But it says he thought she was an intruder?"

"He murdered her."

"Really, you were there? You know what happened?" he snaps, now fully awake.

"He murdered her ... I know."

It is Valentine's Day 2013.

There had been mutterings that "Oscar's not who you think he is ..." Former girlfriends telling stories, friends sharing details of wild times, tales of debauchery. We'd all witnessed his tantrum on the track, the display of bad sportsmanship broadcast across the world when he lost to Brazilian sprinter Alan Oliveira in the 200-metre final at the Paralympics.

And now he's killed Reeva.

Shot her. Four times.

Oscar Pistorius – the Blade Runner, the man who brought the

nation together as he sprinted across the track in his Cheetahs, his prosthetic legs, shaped into those of the fastest animal on earth, dressed in the yellow and green of our country – has slain his girlfriend. The man who we'd cheered as he raised his arm in victory, the tattoo on his left shoulder visible, engraved for all of us to see, "I do not run like a man who is running aimlessly," had fired his weapon and, it seemed, not aimlessly.

We'd forgiven him his previous transgressions. We'd let it go that he had a temper, that he always wanted to win, that he was reckless. But not this time. Not for murder.

And, like millions of others, I am going to demand atonement for this heinous crime.

I'll follow his trial and make sure he doesn't get away with it.

And I do, but as it all plays out, I fall apart.

My life has been crumbling around me for a while, but when I immerse myself in the vague truths, the endless denial, the self-serving lies and the dank deception that emerge during Oscar's court case I am transported back into the opacity of my own past and am left teetering.

As I sit in front of the television, watching for hours, days, weeks and then months, I am unable to pull myself away. And when I'm not watching the trial as it plays out in real time, I record it and view it later, deep into the night, sleep stolen from me as I pause, play and rewind.

It seems the blood of my own hurts is steadily seeping through the bandages of my life and the stains are spreading. I realise that time has only bought distance, that forgetting has not been enough. So, as my wounds suppurate, I take on this murderous matter and, ultimately, it becomes 'Me versus Oscar'.

'Me versus The System.'

And I do not let go.

I follow the testimony of Michelle Burger, the neighbour who had heard a woman's screams, gunshots and then nothing.

I feel her anguish when she is belittled before the court.

"Miss Burger, do you want to be addressed as Miss Burger or Mrs Johnson?" asks the defence advocate.

"My title is Doctor ... but you're welcome to call me whatever you like," she says.

"Madam," snorts the defence without missing a beat, entirely dismissing who she is, "am I right that at least we know one thing about the *context* of your testimony and it is this ... that you stand there believing that Oscar Pistorius lies and that he lied at the bail application?"

His tone suggests that nothing could be more ridiculous or outrageous.

"Your honour, I can only tell you what I heard that night and so I tell it to the court," she replies earnestly.

"Did you understand my question?"

And he repeats that question again and again and again, as though she were a simple, silly woman.

At some point Dr Michelle Burger finally accedes that she hadn't used the words "fear-stricken, petrified" in her original statement. *The fear-stricken, petrified screams of a woman.*

I admire her for sticking to her testimony despite all the attempts to discredit her, suggesting that she is lying or exaggerating before the court. I am disappointed that she doesn't want to be identified on camera. I want to see, know who this courageous woman is. I want to apologise for the way she is being treated.

As the court case continues, I throw myself into the timelines of events and try to piece together what I think really happened. I analyse the contents of the cellphone messages and, alone in front of my TV screen, I dissect them for hours on end. I see the pattern of how Reeva had been placating Oscar and I believe I understand why she had pandered to his moods.

I follow the commentary of the panellists as they deliver their expert opinion between court sessions. I hang onto all their thoughts and opinions, but it is psychologist Leonard Carr, in particular, whom I want to hear. He had been my psychologist during my civil trial, when I needed expert opinion, and as I listen to his measured, insightful responses on TV, I realise that he really understands; he understands the pattern of control, the abuse, the power. I regret that I hadn't really known it all those years ago. As

I watch him, I wish I had trusted him more, been more open to his perceptive thoughts and qualified opinions. Perhaps my healing would have been easier.

So, as I negotiate freedom from my own flashbacks and work to regain control of my life, to find enthusiasm for another tomorrow, I am relieved when it is finally all over, when the verdict is passed.

Then comes the sentencing.

It is outrageous.

Reeva is another woman murdered. Like so many. So many raped and discarded, left for dead, a naked body lying in the open veld. Another woman beaten, bruised and battered. Choked and strangled. Groped on the street. Harassed. Threatened. Another pleading voice not heard. Reeva was murdered in life and now she is being denied in death.

If a convicted murderer, in a matter like this, with the entire world watching, is to spend less than a year incarcerated for his crime, what does that mean for the rest of us?

Why, as women, should we even bother?

What is the point?

Oscar's court case and its outcome tear at the last of my tenuously woven veneer. Listening to the various testimonies and evidence brought before the court, and thinking of Reeva's pain, her bewilderment, and imagining her last, desperate, dying moments, drag me into a choking darkness. I see danger in simple, everyday matters. Just standing beside my husband in the lounge becomes a moment fraught with fear when I realise how he could simply take my head and ram it through the window if he chooses. I know I am being irrational, but I am unable to help myself. My sense of self has disintegrated and, as simple living overwhelms me, I struggle to get through the day without collapsing in a heap and crying for hours.

I am in my car one evening, completely overcome, my head hard against the steering wheel, my sobs punching through me, when my friend Karen calls. I tell her that I don't want to any more, that I can't carry on, that nothing matters any longer.

But for her it does. I matter.

She knows of a remarkable woman, a psychiatrist, who quickly takes me in. But in order for her to help me, I have to remember and I have to tell. In the beginning, it is hard to talk, to reopen old wounds, to pick at crusted scabs, but slowly, as I turn trauma into narrative, I am able to give my story shape. It is through telling that I can ultimately take control of my own life, make sense of it and even try to understand why.

And slowly I journey back into the light to find a new understanding of my worth.

It's been four long years and only now do I feel I can put my story behind me.

This is the last chapter.

And then I will close the book.

One

"You're not allowed here," I warned him.

"I. Don't. Give. A. Fuck."

Those were his words as he lumbered toward me with that loose, loping gait of a tall man. One who has spent a lifetime trying to shorten his stride so that others can keep abreast. He was not a man who could be quiet. His hands were lashing at the air, his shoulders twisting like shifting puzzle pieces. I was trying to put the pieces together, trying to make them fit, not quite certain how. My hands were still suspended, fixed in mid-flick, adjourned, a deferred gesture indicating that he may not enter, when I pressed the remote and soundlessly closed the garage door.

Perhaps he heard my silence because suddenly he calmed, the tension draining from him as his shoulders dropped. He ran his fingers through his tousled fringe and looked down at me with such tenderness.

"I'm so sorry for what I've put you through," he said, tilting his head. "Is there any chance of us getting back together?"

I was quiet.

"Please give me another chance."

I said nothing as I absorbed his now familiar words.

"Don't make me beg ... But I'm asking you to give me another chance."

His voice a little harder, more determined. He was looking down at his feet.

I watched him. I wanted to see the truth in his eyes. I wanted to see whether I could believe him, whether I could trust that this time he truly meant what he said. I wanted to see my pain reflected there. But I couldn't. He was still looking away.

Then suddenly something deep inside me shifted.

I was no longer lost in his dark, brown eyes with their thick, solemn brows. I no longer saw the definition of his chiselled jaw, his high cheekbones or the endearingly flattened tip of his broad nose. As his words melted and morphed, and the last five months moulded as one, his boyish nonchalance, his charm, dissipated.

All I could see were the lies, his disappearing for days without warning, the screaming, the threats, the terror, the hostage-holding, the keeping me up all night, the dragging me through the house by my hair, the choking, the doors locked around me, the phones disconnected, the isolation, the fear and the uncertainty.

I realised that it was never going to change. Never.

As I stood there in my own stillness, I knew that I had been holding onto something that never existed. I finally understood that this could no longer be my journey. I could no longer give credence and value to his distorted perspective.

Was there any chance of us being together? No, there wasn't.

There would never be. Not any more.

It was finally over.

"No, I don't think so," I said softly, trying to find my voice.

I didn't want to anger him.

It took a moment for my words to register, then his face contorted in fury and his rage erupted in a deadly torrent of vile.

"You bitch! You fucking cunt," he screamed. "Give me the fucking air tickets."

He'd bought two air tickets for me and my son to go away for a few days. It was supposed to be a healing getaway, to win me over after the night he'd driven me straight into my garage wall, shouting, "Tonight you're going to die!"

It was an admission of guilt, a bartering for forgiveness, but I had preferred to accept it as a selfless and thoughtful expression of love and apology. He had also sent a bouquet of flowers, which had long since lost their allure and been discarded. The tickets were on my bedside table.

"I'll get them," I said quickly.

It was a short distance to my bedroom, but I moved slowly. I put one foot before the other and trod deliberately away from him. It was only once I was in my bedroom, out of sight, that I rushed forward and reached for the tickets. As I did so I snatched at the remote panic button alongside. I'd recently installed the alarm system and kept the panic button poised and ready just in case. I grabbed it and pressed down frantically, counting, one … two … three.

Not breathing. Four.

I hoped it was long enough to activate the signal, but not long enough to raise his suspicion.

I tossed the panic button aside and bounded back across the room, to the doorway, making up time before slipping back out into the passage. I was still trying to catch my breath as I glided back towards him, eyes lowered. The tickets were in my left hand, carefully caught between thumb and index finger, and I was holding them up high, presenting them ahead of me like a floating, paper peace offering.

But he was having none of it.

He was in the hallway shuffling from one foot to another, immersed in a private dance of rage, as he fuelled his own fury. Somehow, I met his rhythm, instinctively mirroring him, rocking ever so slightly from one side to the other, trying to make myself part of his harmony, trying to placate him, to send out a silent signal that I was not a threat and that I meant no harm. But it was a hollow synchronicity.

As my three-metre journey came to an end I didn't need to look at him, to meet his eyes, to know that his huge, rough hands were splaying and fisting, that his jaw was clenched tight, his teeth grinding. But I lifted my head anyhow and as our eyes locked I saw the shine. I saw how his pupils had brightened with the icy glow of anticipation.

"Please don't," I said, my words nearly silent.
Please don't hit me.
But he did.
He slammed his right fist into my eye.

The pain was instant. I screamed. My hands flew to my face and I spread my fingers wide as I tried to mask myself, but it was too late. He hit me again. I stumbled backwards, but quickly scrambled to my feet and fled to the lounge. I was in the corner, the curtain caught around me, when he upturned the coffee table. I was still screaming when he hoisted the TV cabinet off the floor and hurled it across the room. Then he lunged at me, his hand clamped over my mouth to keep me quiet. But I wouldn't be quiet. He gripped my head and pounded it down into the floor.

He was over me, his face so close to mine that I could feel his spit on my cheek as it sprayed.

"You need your fucking face, don't you?"

I felt the cold glass. A shard from the shattered coffee table, and he was holding it tight against my cheek.

Oh my God! He wants to cut me. Cut my face.

It took everything I had to twist myself from his grip.

And then I ran.

It was my own dance of survival as I dodged him, the broken furniture, and my dog Garp.

I made it past the veranda, back out into the garden, before he caught up and I felt his hands slam down on my back and shoulders. He threw me to the ground and Garp moved in to protect me. I was caught, tied up in a frenzy of my flailing arms, his kicking feet, and a black furry body with a wagging tail. It was impossible to fend off the blows and recoil from wet dog licks at the same time. So I tucked my head in deep, curled up small and hugged myself tight. I left Garp to his nuzzling and him to his heaving, kicking and grunting as I drew my arms in to shield me. Each time I gave in to a strike from his foot I was grateful that he was wearing his brown suede and not his usual heavy, leather boots.

I was still screaming when I heard voices from over the wall. My neighbours.

"Hey, what's going on?"
Shouting. Muffled voices.
"Call the police."
I heard pounding at my door, outside on the street.
"Open up. Open this door!"
Thump. Crack.
I heard the wood splintering and I knew it was over.
I was safe.

I stumbled to my feet and collapsed into the arms of my neighbour and his son. I sagged into them as they carefully lifted me and dragged me through the fractured wooden door. I dropped my head and brought my shaking hands up to hide myself from those who had already gathered on the pavement outside. My shouts had drawn passers-by. There were people standing on the other side of the road. The security guards had arrived and they too stood staring.

My neighbour and his son half dragged, half carried me past the gawking crowd, to the safety of their property. When they placed me gently on a chair it was only then that I looked up at them. They looked the same, both earnest and burly, just many years apart.

The kitchen was a cold, stark room, not the warm, cosy hub expected of a family home. It was immediately obvious there was no woman in the house. The linoleum floor was dated. So too were the chairs, with their spindly steel legs and black rubber tips. Remnants of an era long gone. But the kitchen was spotlessly clean, clinical almost, and I was glad. I didn't want clutter. I wanted space and quiet so that I could try to gather my thoughts.

The son bundled a crumpled, wet dishcloth to my face, and I held it tight to my burning eye. The pain was throbbing through me and the cold cloth pressed against the heat of the swelling brought some relief. He then made sugar water but it sat swirling in the mug. I was unable to hold myself still enough to drink it.

Father and son had raised the alarm when they first heard my screams but the police were yet to arrive. I gave them my sister's number. I knew my mother and her husband, John, were in

Johannesburg for the afternoon and I wanted my sister to contact them so they could be with me.

There was no conversation between us as we sat there, waiting awkwardly. We just stared and waited.

I'd only met my neighbour a week earlier. When I'd knocked on his door, introduced myself and asked him to look out for me, it had been the first time I'd ever seen him. I had shamefully apologised for past disturbances and explained that I had a restraining order in place but that I feared for my safety.

As I sat there trembling, the pain stabbing at my temple, I wondered what would have happened had I not had that prefatory conversation. Would I even be sitting on his chair?

The police finally arrived and we made our way back to my home.

Again I kept myself tucked between my two neighbours. Passers-by still stood waiting and watching over the road and some of my other neighbours had come out too. I saw security patrol vehicles and police vans parked impatiently all along my grass verge.

The armed security guards had somehow prised open what was left of my door and had entered my property. They had also called for backup. Everywhere I turned there seemed to be men in uniform. I heard walkie-talkies and deep, unfamiliar voices.

My home had become a crime scene.

I didn't want to go inside. I didn't want to see all the damage. I already knew that the lounge was strewn with shattered glass, smashed picture frames and ornaments, the splintered remains of furniture. I stayed outside. I left it to my neighbour to manage everyone around me and collapsed onto a chair on the veranda.

I needed to sit.

Garp followed me, but this time, as he moved in closer, there was no wagging tail.

We were both still. His head against my knee, my hand limp against his ear.

I leaned forward and held him tight before burying my head in the cold dishcloth, trying to numb the drilling pain and the horror of all that had happened.

Two

"Where is she? *Where?*" she shouted. "I need to see her!"

I was deep within my own place when I heard my mother's words cut through the white noise that engulfed me. I lifted my head to see her bounding down the stairs toward me, her husband, John, close behind.

"I knew it," she announced to no one in particular. "I couldn't stand him from the moment I first saw him!"

As she moved closer I saw her expression turn from concern to horror. I could see in her eyes what I must look like.

"Look what he's done to you!" she wailed.

But I didn't want to see what he'd done to me.

I already knew.

Once John and my mother were confident that all was being managed efficiently, they quickly bundled me into the car. None of us spoke as we made the short drive through the leafy avenues to Rosebank, to the closest hospital. As the soft hum of the engine eased our silence and we passed the garage and the trendy restaurants with their revelling patrons I sat in the back clutching my eye. My jaw clenched, I was trying hard to keep myself together and saw nothing beyond what was directly in front of me. My mother, her shoulders square, resolutely holding onto the J88 and SAPS 308 forms the police had given her to be completed by the attending district surgeon. John alongside her, his hands firmly on the wheel, sitting tight in the middle of the lane steering us forward, his neck still flushed where his collar creased. John was angry and his parting words at my house played over in my mind.

My phone had rung just as my mother, John and I were heading to the car.

Him.

I had pressed the green button and held my hand open, allowing his invective to effortlessly ricochet around my palm.

His words were rough and coarse.

"You fucking bitch ..."

I had passed my phone to the police officer to bear witness. I then passed it to John.

But John remained completely undeterred by the rant reverberating from the phone, and he joined the shout-down.

"You get to the police station now," John shouted back. "Now!"

Garbled echoes from the handset against John's ear.

"Do you understand me?" John's finger struck at the air. "We will be laying charges."

John was right. We would be laying charges. I would be laying charges. It was the only way, and I was calm in the knowledge that it was procedural and necessary.

John parked the car while my mother and I made our way to Casualty. The automatic doors opened slowly for us to pass through and, as they yawned closed behind us, my mother edged closer. She put her arm around my shoulders and held me tight to her side so we could move through the sterile, dustless air as one. Using her body, she closed me off from prying eyes. I kept my head low, my hands pressed tight to my face. I was trying to block the tears, but I also didn't want to look at anyone. I didn't want to see who bore witness to my shuffle of shame. I didn't want to see anyone showing me pity. But still, as I moved down the passage in my mother's embrace, my shoulders heaving, I felt the unseen glances. I felt them as they pierced and ruptured my back. I heard the silence as I painfully made my way past.

I was immediately ushered through to a ward. Blue curtains were pulled together around me and the next hour became a blur of paperwork and purposeful process. Between the district surgeon, Dr McKenzie, and the nurses, there were many carefully tending hands as they lifted, probed and touched.

"Where does it hurt?" asked Dr McKenzie gently.

"My eye," I said, trying to hold my sobs in.

"Yes, but where else?" she asked, running her hands over me, assessing the damage.

"Don't worry about the rest," I said, pulling my shirt back in place. "It's just my eye."

I was sent for X-rays to check for fractures. There was nothing broken, nothing structural at least.

Dr McKenzie completed the police forms and documented the injuries to my head. According to her report, I had a large supra-orbital haematoma with some right lateral orbital bruising. There was bruising of my anterior neck, left jaw and posterior neck, as well as an injury to my scalp over the occipital lobe. It was all medical jargon, but she noted it word for word.

I left the hospital sedated and a little quieter.

It was dark by the time my mother and John led me into the brightly lit police station.

We were not the only ones there to report a crime.

It was an average Saturday night in a suburban neighbourhood, with regular weekend complaints. A house burglary, a smash-and-grab incident, a broken car window, other petty crime. It was only me who'd been beaten up.

It was busy and there was nowhere to sit. All the seats in the charge office were occupied so we were directed out into the passage, past the peeling, one-way mirror into the overflow area. My mother was still holding me tight as we shuffled through and settled ourselves into the chairs, tufts of hardened yellow foam escaping through the cracks in the blue, faux leather. We waited our turn to make a report.

It was only as I was sitting still in the passage, the medication beginning to numb the pain, that I realised I was shivering, that I was cold. I looked down at the clothes I'd pulled on that morning. Bright green linen shorts, a white T-shirt and shiny takkies. New clothes. I had bought them a few days before. It was a bold outfit, perhaps even a little defiant, suggesting the promise of fresh beginnings. But as I sat there under the harsh fluorescent lighting, my new clothes looked the way I felt. Dirtied, bloodied and rumpled.

I held myself warm, crossing one arm over my chest, my other hand still clutching the wet dishcloth, pressing it flat to my bulging forehead, pushing past the pulsing heat of my swollen eye. It was a pointless gesture. But I tried anyway. I hugged myself close and leaned back against the wall, my head hard against the rough plaster. Walls that had been rubbed smooth from years of other resting heads.

I closed my eyes.

It was all too much.

I didn't want to see what I looked like or where I was. I didn't want to acknowledge the decay, the cracked faux-marble flooring and the grubby electric cables hanging exposed and tired along the grimy walls.

I was stiff from the cold and the pain when his words crashed through, raining down on me.

"Get those motherfuckers out of my sight!" he bawled, his words reverberating down the passage.

It was him. In the charge office.

"Don't let them be near me," he shouted.

I sat upright. I could make out the scuffling and jostling and, although I knew I'd be safe, I backed up into the wall, trying to make myself disappear. I watched as police officers rushed toward him and held him in place. With some force, they managed to form a human cage, a barrier between him and us, out in the passage.

"God forgive me, but he's awful," my mother groaned. "What a dreadful man."

The police officers were having none of it. They restrained him and funnelled him through to the process room somewhere at the back of the station where he was charged with assault and the intent to do grievous bodily harm.

But that was not before I noticed that he had changed.

He was no longer wearing khaki shorts and a T-shirt. Instead he was well turned out: neatly pressed chinos and a fresh white shirt, a navy-blue blazer. Except for his shoes. He was still wearing the same brown suede. He had arrived at the police station cloaked in tailored respectability and was presenting himself as elegant, refined and sophisticated.

I slumped back into my seat, numbed and disbelieving.

Surely not.

It was soon after that we were ushered forward for me to tell my story. I was propping myself up against the tired counter when the policeman who was to take my statement leaned toward me.

His brows came together as he frowned.

He peered closer.

Then his eyes opened in delight and at the top of his voice, loud and clear, his words resonated across the room: "*Hau*, it is YOU!" Leaned a little closer. "It is you. Tracy Going!"

"Yes, it's me," I mumbled.

But he never heard my response as he turned and hollered to his colleague in the adjoining cubicle. His colleague wasted no time and soon the two were standing before me, arms crossed, mouths open wide. They were gaping at me as though I was some wondrous apparition, like it was not possible that I could be there, before them, in real life. They were looking at me as though my forehead was not bulging blue, that my eye wasn't swollen shut, that my hair wasn't hanging limp from the wet dishcloth. They were marvelling.

"You are my role model," the charge officer grinned, shaking his head in disbelief.

"Thank you—" I said.

"*Tjo*, I know that voice," he chuckled. "I listen to you every morning on Radio Metro. You and Bob. *Hau batung*, you two ... You are my favourite."

"Thank you—" I said again.

I couldn't help myself and I smiled.

He was very kind and very generous.

Once the excitement had settled down and everyone around us knew exactly who I was, only then could I proceed with my statement. And it was a long, laborious process. I spoke slowly and clearly. I simplified where I could. I repeated myself when necessary. I spelled out words when needed.

And when we were finally done, I was exhausted. Drained.

All I wanted to do was sleep, and as soon as I was back in the comfort of John's car I folded myself into the leather and surrendered myself to the remainder of the night. I was too scared to be alone, in too much pain, couldn't face the destruction in my home, so I went back with my mother and John.

As the streetlights broke through the darkness, we made our way down Jan Smuts Avenue and headed out to Brits. I let the soft classical notes of John's music wash over me, and soon the strobes between the lampposts lessened and finally ceased.

"We're not letting this go," I heard my mother's soft murmurs. "She can't allow anyone to do this to her and get away with it."

Her voice was faint and although her words emerged distorted, fading in and out of my understanding as the plop of tyre fused with the tar, I knew she was right. But I couldn't bring myself to think about my immediate future. Not now. So, instead, I allowed the blackness to swallow me up until I no longer saw the stars pricking the sky outside like trillions of sharp needles.

I closed my eyes and tried to still my thoughts.

I needed a warm, soaking bath to soothe my aching body but when we arrived it was more than I could manage so instead I took some more painkillers and eased myself into my childhood bed.

"Try to get some sleep" were my mother's words. "We'll talk in the morning," she said.

It had been a lifetime since she'd last tucked me in and I found it comforting. I lay there quiet and unmoving, hoping that the stillness would clear my mind so that I could forget and rest. It was a pitiful pretence, for sleep eluded me.

Three

I knew I was awake – and I didn't want to be. I longed to be wrapped up in the warmth of oblivion. I wanted to undo the day before. I wanted it never to have happened. But I couldn't. I knew that. Nothing would ever change it.

My childhood bedroom had long since been redecorated. Gone was the cobalt-blue feature wall. It was all floral now, pink and flowery. John had arrived in my mother's life with his heavy, dated furniture and there had been nowhere else to put it all. So now my old bedroom was dwarfed by its interior. I lay still, only my eyes moving as I glanced around. It was far too busy for my comfort. One wall was framed solid with a built-in cupboard that my father had crafted many years before, the other wall compressed with John's two free-standing closets, held apart by a matching, and equally oppressive dressing table.

I couldn't breathe.

It was as though the air that threaded between all the furniture had pressed tight together around me, musty and dark. As though the past was clinging desperately to the ball-and-claw feet, hanging on tight like a sad, fading memory. It was a room that had been allowed to stagnate. It was a room that was no longer used.

I lay still, trying not to move my head, trying not to provoke the pain, trying to keep my mind as static as the air around me so that my thoughts wouldn't push through. But they did. They swirled and eddied until they won.

How did I get here?

Where had it all gone wrong?

I played it over in my mind. The day before had started out as any ordinary weekend day. It was a Saturday, which meant I had slept in long past sunrise. This was a luxury I *permitted* myself, given that Monday to Friday I catapulted from my bed and rushed to the studio of the biggest commercial radio station in the country. Each weekday morning at six, as the digital clock blinked its exactness in red numbers on the studio wall, I woke up millions of listeners and brought them the first news bulletin of the day in what I liked to think of as my perky, crisp and articulate manner. But Saturdays were different. Saturdays were leisurely. There was no need to rush anywhere.

My son was with his father for the weekend. The day had been mine.

It was the twenty-fifth day of October 1997 and spring had finally reached its sell-by date. The morning had gone quickly and soon passed into afternoon. I had spent most of my time out on the veranda pretending to read, but the words had washed right over me. I had tried to concentrate but it was difficult, distracted as I was by all that had happened over the preceding weeks. So mostly my book lay neglected beside me. It had been far less demanding to squander time watching a hummingbird play a solitary game of tag between the leaves of the *Aloe africana* in the far corner of my garden than it had been to try to concentrate, to absorb words on a page. I had sat there watching mindlessly, hypnotised by the mundanity of it frantically flitting from one tubular pendant to another, a magnificent blur of jewelled feathers. The hummingbird, just like me watching it, both of us lost in the aloe's succulent pride as it nonchalantly flouted the constraints of grass and gridded paving. The aloe, standing tall, boasting orange-red pokers like an aide-mémoire that life must be lived in profusion despite the season.

I had been trying to do that too.

My sister had popped around for a visit. One of those

impromptu visits I had come to expect. She'd been by my side the last few weeks, watching me, phoning me, protecting me, even sleeping over occasionally, not wanting to leave me on my own for too long, afraid that something else might happen. We had talked about nothing and everything. We had drunk tea.

It was soon after she left that the ringtone of my phone broke the silence.

It was him.

I had watched it ring a few times before swiping at the green button, standing up as though I was shrugging off my fright, tossing aside my fear, like a coat I needed to escape, not yet used to its weight.

I had listened to him as he explained that he was outside my house, down on the street. The same street that had offered me no refuge a few weeks earlier. The one I had fled down late at night, my jacket hanging torn from my back, as I tried to get away from him. He was out there again.

"Please, I need to talk to you," he said, his voice low and desperate.

It was the third time he had phoned in the past hour.

"You know we can't see each other," I said, as though to remind him.

It had been three weeks since the family court interdict had been implemented. I had secured a restraining order, a piece of paper that prevented him from being anywhere near me or my property. It stated clearly that he was not allowed to threaten me or harm me in any way, nor was he allowed to make any contact.

When the sheriff of the court served the papers on him, he'd laughed.

"Not worth the paper it's written on," he'd scoffed.

But he'd left me alone.

Then he phoned.

I ignored it.

He phoned again.

And again.

I broke the restraining order as I answered.

I listened as he gave me the words I so desperately wanted to hear. Needed to hear.

I'm sorry. I didn't mean to do it.

Then he phoned daily, hourly even. Court records would later show it was fifty-eight times. Always apologising, often coaxing, sometimes shouting and threatening. I had taken his calls then just as I had taken his call the day before.

The first bruises had long faded and although I was still confused by his anger and unpredictability, I had become increasingly lulled by his endless calls of remorse and regret, the flowers, the air tickets and the offers to repair and pay for damages to my property.

His words, his kindness, his generosity, were making me feel whole again.

I didn't want to believe that I was caught in a vortex of destruction.

I wanted to believe that I was above that, that I was more.

And for this I needed him to explain it all away, to minimise it, so that I could rationalise my horrible hurt. I needed his reassurance of a new beginning, and the certainty of a promised shift in his behaviour. I wanted him to look me in my eyes and ask for my forgiveness so that I could validate my worthiness.

I wanted to understand ... and to ask why.

Why?

Why had he done this to me? To us?

Why?

As I had stood quietly on my veranda, listening to his desperation, his brokenness, I wanted his answers.

"Please—" he said. "I need to talk to you."

As his words tumbled out, I allowed time to stand still. I let it stretch around me as I heard all that I wanted to hear. I was holding my phone tight, as tight as the sun was holding onto the day. I would drop my phone just as the sun would ultimately lose its grip, but for then it hadn't. It had been so easy to reason my way through it ... There was no darkness to shield him ... It was light. He was on the other side ... in municipal no-man's land ... neutral territory. Surely, I'd be safe. Surely?

I collapsed into that dark, grey, mouldy expanse of wrongness.

"I'll come out to you," I'd said. "I'll be there now."

Those were my words as I stood tall, back straight, like the aloe in the corner of my garden. I too prided myself on being centred, balanced and strong, rooted in my strength as a young, successful mother and woman.

It had taken no time at all to find my new, white takkies.

But as I bent down to slip them on I knew I wasn't really as strong as I hoped. I knew my boldness was a fragile thing and that it was already beginning to disintegrate as I hurriedly knotted my laces.

It was then that I executed the very smallest of motions, an almost imperceptible gesture that left no indent in the hardened plastic casing of the remote for the garage door. Just an invisible thumbprint. But nothing is ever truly invisible.

I opened the garage door ... and he slipped in. I rushed forward, my fingers flicking pathetically in the afternoon air, gesturing to him not to enter my property, reminding him that I'd said I was coming out. But he'd already cut the distance between us with no more than a few easy strides.

I played the conversation over in my head.

"You're not allowed here."

And I heard his response again and again: "I don't give a fuck."

And with reflection, he was so right.

He didn't. He really didn't.

◯

The knock on the door brought me back. My mother.

"Good morning," she said, peering cautiously around the door, holding a cup of tea. "Can I open the curtains a bit?"

"No," I mumbled, trying not to move my face.

"How you feeling?"

"Sore," I said, indicating for her to leave the tea on my bedside table.

She nodded knowingly.

It was the only sign she gave – and we would never speak of it again.

As the tea grew cold, I lay unmoving.

I tried to block the light from my eyes, but it persisted and filtered through where the curtain fell away from the window. It wasn't a bright, illuminating splinter of whiteness. More a separation of light from the dark. But still it penetrated. It split my thoughts and suspended me between time and place.

I knew as I lay in my old bed that if the best of all possible worlds was *choice* then I would never have come back. I had very little heart for this place. Sometimes it's best to leave behind that which is over, but as I quietened myself it came to me that there never really are endings. Endings are a deception. Endings are not defined. They are arbitrary and inconclusive.

It was unnerving to know that, ultimately, I had not left; that instead what had taken me from this house had brought me right back.

Four

I was five-and-a-half years old when we moved to the first house my father built. It was the year my family relocated from the Cape to the Transvaal. It was here in Ana Landbouhoewes, thirteen kilometres outside of Brits, that my father found himself a plot of dehydrated land and bought it as his own.

I have no understanding of what about the place had truly resonated with him. Perhaps he was drawn to the concrete reservoir with its thick sludge that hung heavy over the water like a velvet mirage, offering a false promise of quenching the thirst of its surrounds. That he saw his own dream of settling when he happened upon the stone workers' hut that offered some respite in the far corner, close to the boundary fence. There was nothing else to redeem those few hectares of land, just the reservoir and the workers' hut, its walls burnt black from the daily wood fire. So maybe that's all it was for my father; possibility, the prospect of new beginnings and our very own story that took us all from everything we knew to a place we had to negotiate and a language we had yet to learn.

Looking back, it was my mother who embraced our new way of life most readily.

My memory of her is of someone who seemed unfazed by the challenge, who fearlessly took to taming the veld around us. She had been born and raised in the heart of the Karoo, a land of arid air and cloudless skies, it could have been because she simply understood the brutality of the land and unflinchingly submitted herself to its harshness. Or maybe she believed that, just as the dried *tolbos* was swept in on the afternoon Highveld dust storms, to be tossed around before being flirtatiously flicked in the air as the wind took its aim, her life too would tumble in another direction. Either way, she knew to persist and had soon cleared the hem of the house, cut back the long, parched grass and provided us with a garden of roughly strewn stones and rocks.

Over the following two years these stones and rocks would be painstakingly collected and stacked for my father to eventually build us a permanent house a few hundred yards away. But first my father built us a grand shack with shallow foundations and uneven, concrete floors.

He, along with Charlie – who seemed to be born of the land and was there when my father first arrived – had built our temporary abode, wooden slat for wooden slat. Charlie would set aside his carved walking stick before hitching his oversized trousers into his waist, and together with my father they would sweat, saw and persevere as one to finally produce a structure suitable to be called home. As the night descended and it became too dark to drive another nail, Charlie would slip away and leave my father to breathe deep on his Texan Plains. He would sit content, as the rings of smoke from his cigarette curled through the night air to blend with the malty sweetness of his Lion Lager, satisfied that the profile of the landscape was changing just as he'd envisioned.

It didn't take long for our squat, timber square to take shape. We – my mother, the twins and I – arrived to see it standing, splendid with its flat, corrugated-iron roof, its four cut-out steel windows and its hinge-panel front door. As we entered we needed to adjust our eyes to peer into the darkness. The interior had been divided roughly in two by way of untreated wood partitioning.

My mother placed the Sanderson couch in the front section, clearly dividing the lounge from the allocated dining area; further back was the kitchen and alongside it the bathroom. The bathroom was partially separated, allowing for at least some form of unlit privacy, but was too small to host the metal tub that was our bath. Every evening the tub took centre stage as my mother dragged it to the middle of the kitchen and a quarter filled it with pot-boiled hot water, before the squirming bodies of my brother, my sister and I were squeezed in. This not only saved on time for my mother but also simultaneously raised the level of the water. Our collective howls of objection would fill the kitchen as she grabbed at our feet and, with a hard brush, scrubbed the dirt that had become one with our soles. No child wore shoes on this side of the world.

To the left of the wooden room divider was where we slept. The front part had been half closed in for my parents, the back area a dark cavernous space with three beds lined up alongside each other like skittles. Given that I was the eldest, I was afforded the privilege of choosing my bed first, so the bed on the left became mine. It was a good spot to have as it was the closest to the light – and the closest to my parents. The twins fought it out between themselves for the next best spot. My brother won.

My father, being a practical man and one of great ingenuity, saw the pine panelling that separated us from the living area as a perfect storage opportunity. Stacked high up along the top shelf were the Afrovan removal boxes that would be unpacked only when needed. Those boxes on the ground stood much taller than me, and when arranged above me they loomed large like skulking monsters that came to devour children as they slept. During the day I stored away the gnawing fear, but as the night settled in, ominous shapes began to take form between the shadows of those imposing cartons. I would lie there frozen, frightened and breathless, telling myself that the folded blanket was not a python coiled and ready to strike. But I was never able to believe it. My eyes were fixed on the serpent, too scared to blink in case it moved and then disappeared, only to reappear as it slithered over me and covered me in the dust of its scales.

Snakes became a part of our new lives. My brother, my sister and I would soon learn to identify one serpent from another, but thankfully nobody ever needed to use the antivenom stored in the fridge next to the milk. Puff adders were by far the most prevalent and it took my father, his .22 rifle and many armfuls of cartridges to try to destroy the nest of vipers that were breeding unconstrained under the rocks alongside the reservoir. My mother stood at a distance, shouting words of warning.

"Bruce! Be careful!"

"There's another one behind you."

And there was.

And another.

One puff adder after the other, writhing and undulating as they intertwined.

It was Charlie, with his stick, who taught us to listen for their *puff*, to always look down as we walked and to recognise their cryptic colouration as they lounged lazily, carefully camouflaged in their natural habitat. It was also Charlie who came rushing to the back door one afternoon, ashen in pallor, shouting for my mother.

"*Miessies!*"

My mother opened the door, eyes wide.

"*Daar's 'n slang! 'n Groot slang!*"

Eyes wider still.

"*Ek kannie die kop of'ie stert sien nie!*" he yelled, his stick hanging useless at his side.

I never did see the snake that stretched from the one side of the road to the other, obscuring both its head and tail at the same time. But I knew it as the python that lived in the hollow beneath the marula tree, the one that guarded the bottom gate, and from then on we were no longer allowed to wait under the tree for my father to come home from work.

We checked our beds at night to make sure that no cobra had tucked itself in. We kept our eyes open for mambas, by far the most deadly, and lost a bit of ourselves when our dog, Spekkie, died of one's poison. We watched out for rinkhals that played dead. We observed the boomslangs as they warmed themselves out in the sun or became one with the branch, still and unmoving.

But the most spectacular was the snake that would one day make its way down our slate passage. It was school holidays and it was just my brother, David, and I at home when it made its magnificent entrance. My brother was in the passage when it sashayed toward him, its head swaying from side to side. I was in the kitchen frying our favourite slap chips when David ran in screaming. I couldn't make out his words. I thought he'd been stung by a bee. He was very allergic.

"It's okay," I said, "Calm down."

"No. It's a python!" he screamed.

A python?

"Johanna!" I shouted. "*Daars 'n slang – kom gou!*"

Johanna tossed her iron aside and came running.

"*Dis onner die couch, Johanna!*"

"*Nee, nonnie, hy'sie daarie,*" she said peering into the under-couch darkness.

And then, as she dropped the couch back into place, it slithered out from under it, shifty eyes darting, tongue flicking. It was the biggest snake I had ever seen. Easily three metres long and as wide as my hand. So big that we couldn't kill it. We managed, though, to close it in the TV room.

Then I leapt up onto the dining table, not wanting my feet touching discarded scales, and called my father.

The snake park sent one of its handlers. It turned out not to be a python after all. It was a banded Egyptian cobra. And that was how our very own cobra was given its own glass cage next to the prized king cobra at the park. Our snake then became the second biggest snake I'd ever seen and we were given complimentary entrance to the snake park for as long as everyone remembered.

As scorpions and spiders also blended seamlessly into our environment, my mother decided it was time to introduce animals that we might prefer. So my father and Charlie set to constructing cages and pens and hutches and soon we had chickens, ducks and rabbits. We got stuck in – feeding, collecting eggs and counting bunnies. But the most anticipated event of the year was the spring arrival of three fluffy white lambs, one for each of us to hand rear. We eagerly took ownership of our little lambs and gave them meaningful names like Fluffy, Snow and Diane. We held them tight as they greedily drank the milk that foamed from teats attached to Coke bottles. We wrestled with them, spent hours training them to follow us and generally loved them until they became big, robust sheep with woolly, matted coats. It was heartrending when they mysteriously disappeared, one by one. My father said it was the jackals.

Charlie fashioned out a vegetable patch and soon we were growing our own vegetables too, leafy lettuces, spinach, carrots and cabbages. Aside from the bird coop, the vegetable patch and the cleared rock garden, the veld around us was an impenetrable expanse. It was dense with waist-high shrubs, thorn trees, aloes and proteas, a vast wildness that became our playground.

We had no immediate neighbours – or at least none that we could see from the house – and, having moved from Port Elizabeth, it was a surprise to realise that people could live so far apart. The Bothas owned the smallholding to our right and we only saw them when we passed each other occasionally on the dust road. It was a road that needed to be graded annually after the rains, an initiative spearheaded by Mr Botha himself as he preferred a smoother surface for his Mercedes-Benz. Mr Botha was a distinguished man, active in the local municipality and involved in the church. Mrs Botha was equally refined. To our distant left Johann, the hairdresser, and his boyfriend lived discreetly. Almost two kilometres away, toward the national road, were the Bezuidenhouts, whom we would only befriend once we started catching the school bus. Then on the other side, even further away, were the Van der Merwes and the Du Toits. It would take years for the Goings to integrate.

But if there was one thing that brought the entire community of Ana Landbouhoewes together quickly, it was a veld fire. And we were particularly vulnerable in our wooden tinderbox. It wasn't just the time my brother set a match to the grass; the blazing sun had a habit of taking its vengeance out on the parched ground, and its blistering heat was enough for the grass to self-ignite and start a wave of destruction that could quickly escalate out of control. There was one particular night when it seemed that Vulcan himself had released his fury in the form of an almighty blaze that almost took us with him.

We awoke to find our bedroom lit up bright orange. I remember screaming for my mother, but she wasn't there. All human effort was needed to battle that fire and the calming of three distraught children was not a priority. We huddled together as we listened to the echoes of panic.

"Oppas!"
"Gaan daardie kant!"
"Kry nog water!"
"Gou! Die wind het gedraai."

The flames were raging tall, higher than our house, plundering everything in their path. We could hear the fire rushing towards us, its noise deafening as it pitched and peaked. As the God of Fire and Forge fiercely continued its rampage and the air around us closed in with a blazing heat, my brother, my sister and I held each other tight. We listened to the sound of wet branches being battered into the ground, melding into the thud of sodden hessian bags as neighbours from all around tried to beat back the raging furnace. By the time the fire engines arrived from town, the smell of burning acacias had long since filled our lungs. But the fight was far from over – it took the rest of the night before the fire was contained and days more before the smouldering embers had burnt themselves out.

The veld around us reclaimed its structure slowly as weakened roots strengthened and small creatures returned. It was a tentative process of healing and a daily reminder that life was fragile and that all dangers needed to be contained.

Five

Brits was built on the back of the motor-manufacturing industry, sweating miners, subsidised farmers and staunch Afrikaner politics. It was in fact just outside Brits, at the nearby De Wildt railway station, that the heart of the National Party first beat following a speech by General Barry Hertzog in 1912. It was a town proud of its heritage and, as cultural purity reigned, it comfortably gave prominence to those more radical in their views.

Dries Alberts lived near the Hartbeespoort Dam, where when the sluices opened the waters rushed to nourish the surrounding farmlands. It was here that the wheelchair-bound chief of publicity for the Afrikaner Weerstandsbeweging (AWB) spewed his propaganda. As a committed supporter of separate development, it was reported, he insisted on only the purest Afrikaans being spoken in his home. It seemed a great irony that he inflicted an English education on his hapless daughter and that we would eventually attend the same school. I remember her as an achingly shy young woman with big, burnt-umber eyes that opened wide as though always startled, and a caring, gentle smile. Her long plait fell like a twisted rope, well past her broadened hips, and hung heavy, a constant reminder that she was desperately out of her cultural depth.

Then closer to Brits, a stone's throw from where we lived, was the stalwart and former wrestler Manie Maritz. In the late afternoons, he would grandly traverse his land, sitting straight and tall on his horse as he admired his Brahman cattle grazing nonchalantly in the veld, the entire herd completely oblivious to his supremacy. His rifle was always firmly lodged at his side as he patrolled his perimeter fence. A formidable force in khaki. The only hint of colour to break my memory was the insignia, the three black sevens that formed a triskelion in a white circle, conspicuous on a red background and worn openly on his sleeve.

But Brits was founded nearly seventy years before we arrived and we got there to find it leaning out of the shadows of its very modest railway-station beginnings. The town had risen out of the dust as businesses started up on the southern side of the train lines, on a road called Tom Street. Those businesses had since relocated north, across the line, and when I first knew Tom Street the scent of fresh Indian spices masked the dank smell of empty buildings and the richness of ground roots and desiccated bark filled the air. Shops opened onto the street, loud music beckoned, smiling faces greeted and owners and their sons lilted, "Good price. Good price."

"Excellent price."

"No worries, my cousin over the road will have your size. Let me call him."

"Cheap-cheap."

It was a street filled with special spices, sumptuous silks and bargain-basement buys.

The formal sector, where the more earnest business was done, had evolved over the years and Brits central was a sprawl of single-storey buildings that stretched from Spoorweg Street to the Town Hall. There the colour of saris was replaced by khaki, veldskoens and crimplene. Only lawyers, teachers and politicians wore suits, ties, long socks or pantyhose in that heat.

Ou Kasie, marginalised on the outskirts of town and hidden from view over the hill, was where resilience reigned and the burgeoning black community resided.

We all had our place in the sun, somewhere between God and the community, and there was no need for anything beyond. If someone died, everyone cared. If you got lost, then you'd be found. If you did well at school, the *Brits Pos* reported on it. It was a place where open secrets were shared and where dark secrets festered.

The author Brenna Yovanoff once wrote that the simple truth of a town is that you can know and love and hate it or even blame it and resent it, but nothing will change it – and that, ultimately, you're just another part of it.

We were just another part of Brits.

We had been there just on two months when I started Grade 1 at the local primary school, Laerskool Brits. We woke up really early that morning. My mother buttoned me up in my new yellow shirt and then pulled the square-necked, green dress with its firm flounce over my protesting head before getting the twins ready for their first day at the adjacent *kleuterskool*. When I climbed out of the car I pulled my short, green socks up long and high over my calves, trying to cover myself, all the while clutching my new cardboard suitcase. I walked in with it bumping against the back of my legs. My lunchbox and pencil case knocked around hollowly inside. I was just as hollow as I met Mrs Hickey and received the first of her daily hugs. Once all the parents had left, with lingering looks and the last of hugs, Mrs Hickey lined us all up and, holding hands, we snaked our way to the quad to stand together and sing for *Volk en Vaderland*. As the orange, white and blue flag was hoisted heavenward, our headmaster Mr Botha – said to be the nephew of the then Minister of Foreign Affairs, Pik Botha – placed his hand on his heart and led the way.

I was one of fourteen English-speaking pupils in Grade 1. It was an intake so large and so significant that the *Brits Pos* reported on it. The article went on to expound that had two additional students entered the system it would have warranted the appointment of another teacher, bringing the tally to five. But given that we fell short by two, nothing changed and it seemed four would have to do. The piece also announced my mother as a new teacher, but it failed to detail who she had replaced. It was an auspicious start to my school career.

The English-medium classes were separated from the main body, mostly into stuffy, prefabricated rooms where we were convinced we would choke and ultimately succumb to a torturous death of mesothelioma as we inhaled invisible asbestos filaments, either in the sweltering heat or with our knees knocking helplessly in the biting cold. It was here, sliced between the netball courts and the rugby veld overlooking the railway line and the silos, that we were schooled. It was an inconvenience not by design but rather from necessity as little provision had been made for the English arriving in Brits. The classes were so few in numbers that sometimes three grades would be taught in one class by a single teacher. My mother became one of those teachers.

My mother was a formally educated woman with a diploma in teaching. My father was not. He had fled boarding school in his penultimate year to never officially complete his education. But despite how qualified – and how respected – my mother was, and despite the long hours she sacrificed preparing, teaching and marking for three grades simultaneously, because she was not Afrikaans, it was necessary for her to reapply for her post annually. This uncertainty brought significant stress to our home, especially as my father's need to seek oblivion in alcohol deepened and he became increasingly unreliable and unpredictable. And so it was that my mother's level of education became a convenient and deliberate weapon of contention in the home.

Education and religion. Nothing more was required.

My mother being clever and her relationship with God. This was enough to unleash the rage.

Over the years it became a finely honed script. My father would come home late into the night, long after we were in bed. I would hear the argument start, then bear witness to its gradual and predictable escalation. My father belligerent, my mother pleading. As their voices rose, I would cup my ears closed, not wanting to hear, while I dug myself deeper into the bedding.

"You-shink-you-so-clever," he'd slur.

"No, I'm not."

"Yesh-you-are! Look't-you – a know-it-all!" he'd shout.

"No, I don't, I don't know it all," she'd beg. "Please. Please,

Bruce, don't. The children. The children are sleeping."

It always started the same. Ended the same. The thumping. The pushing. The wrestling. Then the fists. Always the same. As I lay there with the air drawn from my bedroom, I would grab my blanket closer and place my thumb in my mouth, tears flushing my cheeks.

Afterwards, as the quietness pounded like the calm after a thunderstorm, I'd listen hard for the sound of her crying. When I heard it, I could take comfort knowing I hadn't been abandoned and that my mother was still alive.

When I woke in the mornings my bed was wet and cold.

By the time I was washed and dressed, the overturned furniture was back in place and whatever had been destroyed set aside. We'd have breakfast and make our way to school, my mother taking special care to dress in order to hide her welts and bruises.

There were mornings that she didn't manage to get to work at all, like the time my father cracked her head open with an empty Lion Lager bottle. By then we were already making use of the school bus so, after the early-morning ritual, she could return home to soak the blood from her matted hair and make her way back to bed to allow the hurts to heal.

Otherwise, as the day broke, she usually woke us up cheerfully and just as the weak rays of the sun melted the dew and the dank smell of moist sand tainted the air, we would clamber onto the bus for the lengthy journey through the farms of De Kroon to town. It was an old bus that rumbled along, detonating gravel rudely behind it. Each time it rolled to a stop to collect more scholars, clouds of dust would overtake us and our mouths would taste the grit as we stared out the window, our eyes still itchy from sleep. We always sat in the same place, behind the driver, in the front row. My brother, my sister and me next to each other, blonde and blue-eyed. Invariably, much bullying, shoving and pushing happened behind us, especially between the high-school boys, but the three of us sat there immune, safe, untouched and seemingly protected. We were English. And our mother, after all, was a teacher at the school.

But all privilege immediately dissolved when we were dropped off in the afternoons and made our way home along the dirt road. To break the tedium of our kilometre walk it sometimes became a game of neighbours pitted against neighbours and then we'd all gleefully and viciously participate in our very own post-Boer War flare-ups.

And this was just the place to do it, right here in the foothills of the Magaliesberg, deep in the valley of Silkaatsnek, where Generaal Koos de la Rey had played his hand and where the British Colonel Frederick Roberts had raised a white flag in defeat on that eleventh day of July 1900.

As our neighbours, the Badenhorsts, celebrated that long-ago victory, we took up the cause for Colonel Roberts and unreservedly fought back with stones that were thrown to almost miss and insults that were not fully understood.

"*Engelsman!*" they shouted.

"Dutchmen!" we hollered.

"*Jy's 'n rooinek. 'n Soutie.*"

"You're a plank. A *houdkop*."

It made for an exhilarating journey home.

Other days were less eventful. Then we strolled along together, talking, laughing and kicking at the dirt. Some afternoons we stopped to pat the cows. Mostly, the cows ignored us and it became a competition of who could lure a brave one through the fence first and then stand still long enough as it enveloped a hand and an arm with its long tongue like a sandpaper tentacle all wet, sticky and slobbery.

But, together, we always looked out for snakes and we never fought on weekends and definitely not during school holidays.

Then we were steadfast friends.

Six

We stopped pretending that my father didn't have a drinking problem at about the same time the Badenhorsts moved in to the smallholding alongside us. It wasn't so much us no longer looking for hidden bottles, but rather that he simply stopped hiding them.

There had been a *special* on at the local bottle store, an alluring offer too seductive to snub. It's a mystery as to how we afforded it, and as children do, we sniggered that perhaps a drought was imminent. My father arrived home with cases and cases and cases of Lion Lager. With a bent back and great fervour, he had heaved them in and stacked them meticulously and methodically, one above the other, all along the walls of the only unused room in our new stone house. Our spare bedroom was quickly converted into a lofty castle of lager, an effigy to alcohol. It was so impressive that we soon invited our new neighbours to witness it. This stupendous viewing cemented our acquaintance and a great time was spent together building castles within this grand, imposing structure. We strung blankets between sixpacks and used the towering columns of beer crates as our turrets.

Our lives took on a sparkle when the Badenhorsts arrived. Johann, the hairdresser, and his boyfriend had departed as discreetly as they had lived, but there was nothing restrained about the arrival of the Badenhorsts. They announced themselves on the land; Mr and Mrs Badenhorst and their four children moved in lock, stock and barrels of birds, and dogs, and broken vehicles that were left stationary wherever they had been dragged, rusted and ruined car parts framing their resting place. Gradually, over time, the tractor arrived, then the scramblers, the peacocks, the pigs, the cows and the endless swarms of flies.

Mr Badenhorst, Oom Baadie, was a short, corpulent man with a wide girth that challenged his height for span. And as is so often the case with round people, he seemed constantly out of breath as he rushed along. His dark hair, carefully Brylcreemed back into glistening curls, emphasised a wide, pulpy face, usually pink from exertion. And with his thick lips fixed in a beaming smile, he was all set for a sonorous *"Kom gee vir oom 'n soëntjie"*.

But my sister and I didn't much care for Oom Baadie's stubble brushing our soft cheeks.

Before we were aware of the python nestled within the sun-baked hollow of the marula tree at the lower gate, in the times when we still waited for my father to come home at dusk, we would be sitting perched on the stone wall, our faces aglow with the dusty shine of a setting sun, when we'd hear the cheerful chortle of Oom Baadie's painstakingly preserved Volkswagen Beetle. With our knees bent and toes grabbing at rough, rocky edges for grip, we'd follow his journey as he paused at the entrance to his farm, and then corrected his course and veered toward us. But we really had no need for a clammy kiss and we soon learnt to hide within the leafy crown above us as we kept an eye on the halo of dust announcing his amorous approach.

Yet, despite his rotund shape, Oom Baadie was a man neat in appearance, typically dressed in blue. It was cobalt blue, the colour of a blue-collar worker. With the motor industry the mainstay of our town's economy, there was much demand for skilled mechanics and Oom Baadie was employed by the largest tyre-manufacturing company in the area. It seemed that he wore his blue overalls with pride, overalls that would undoubtedly have been shortened by Mrs Badenhorst.

Mrs Badenhorst was quiet and reserved, and usually to be found in her dimly lit kitchen or behind her Singer sewing machine. She was also much, much taller than her husband.

The arrival of the young Badenhorsts – Jannie, Andries, Marie and Dirk – made a measurable difference to our happiness. They provided the social connection that we craved. Suddenly, we were no longer so isolated. Perhaps it was the same for them as we tore across the veld in the rush to get from one house to the other.

Jannie, being the oldest, looked out for us all.

Andries was a chip off the old proverbial 'block', a mirror to his father's face, although not yet stout. He attended the same school as us, except he was in the *special* class. It seemed that he was a bit *slow*, and the only way the family could successfully communicate with him was to raise their voices. Andries was always being shouted at.

It was well after dark and I was warm in my bed when Oom Baadie's bellows breached the quiet of one particular night. Someone had forgotten to latch the pigsty – clearly, it was Andries – and the pigs were out. What followed was an almighty commotion. As the human-like noise of squealing pigs swelled the sky, it became difficult to differentiate between the sound of man and beast. However, between the howls, heaves and grunts, Oom Baadie managed to raise his voice sufficiently to holler a hoarse, "*Andries, vang die vokken vark!*"

This was followed by a breathless, taut, "*Kannie, Pa!*"

"*Vokken vang hom nou!*"

There is no easy way to catch a pig.

Especially in the dark.

Eventually, once all had been rounded up, captured and impounded, and I had stopped giggling, the night resumed its familiar stillness and I fell asleep.

Perhaps it was also Andries who forgot to latch the aviary.

It was a sunny Sunday afternoon – and hot, too hot for even the bleached grass to move. We were ensconced indoors, trying to escape the swelter, when a trilling, shrieking cacophony alerted us to yet another imminent adventure centred around the Badenhorsts. We rushed out to find a squalling mass of partially pinioned birds, flapping frantically above. It was a veritable migration happening right over our veranda. It didn't take long to realise that it was in fact the Badenhorsts' collection of budgies and canaries that had taken to the air. We, naturally, added to the stridency as my brother, sister and I leapt about, heads held high, and grabbed at winged silhouettes. Oom Baadie's voice resonating across the veld added to our fervour. We congratulated ourselves as we caught two little yellow canaries and one large blue budgie, which we shamelessly caged for ourselves.

Marie was the only daughter. She and I were close enough in age to spend much time with our heads together, her cropped hair falling forward over cheeks dusted with freckles, as we dressed our Barbie dolls, mostly in gowns that we fashioned ourselves. It was a gentle friendship. Marie was soft and kind and would have done well growing up in town.

Dirk was much younger than me, and we didn't spend much time together.

But otherwise, between ourselves, we hewed a happy childhood from that open veld as we climbed trees, built makeshift treehouses, sprained limbs, and cracked chins.

We learnt to swim.

We rode our bikes.

The bikes would eventually be set aside once we were older and taller, and then we took to 125cc Suzuki scramblers and the disused quarry a few kilometres away. It was there that Jannie, the younger Bezuidenhout brother and my brother, David, would throttle it out, blasting granite deposits as they raced the grey dunes. Lapping each other, trying to be the fastest. Us girls, glittered in the gravelly dust, would scream with delight as we hung on tight on the back with our legs bandied, trying to keep clear of the exhaust and its incinerating touch.

We learnt to shoot, mostly with our pellet guns and less often with the .22 rifle and its live ammunition. Target practice usually happened at our house. We would place our targets evenly along the knee-high stone wall, just behind the flowerbeds, and pretend it was the boundary to our garden fort. We would lie low and swat the grass from our noses as we leopard-crawled into position. Then, as we nuzzled the gun in our armpits, we'd line up the scope, take aim and fire, careful to avoid the dahlias and geraniums. Our garden was the biggest so it made sense to shoot there, but what was also convenient was that there was never a shortage of targets at our house. We offered an unlimited supply of Lion Lager cans.

And my father was emptying them, drinking them ... fast. As fast as he could. Faster than we could shoot a bull's-eye through the O of *Lion*.

He was often at home and had begun to adopt more flexible working hours as he fell deeper and deeper into the clutches of alcoholism. The binges were now more intense and the time between them less. As he slumped down into his armchair, he had become one with our afternoons. He would sit there in the dark, with the lounge curtains drawn, casting his own shadow. It was only the ash that stirred as it grew steadily and then fell from the glowing tip of his Texan Plain, hung limp in his hand. Until the next beer. Then the brash silence of the suck as the seal was broken, as if the beer was drawing its first air, before exhaling, and burping its decay. My father, with his glazed gaze, sat there staring, completely fixated on the pull. As the afternoon continued, and as his mind dulled in its prelude to oblivion, his bald head would loll forward, until the stupor inevitably yielded and he passed out.

I was ashamed of my father, the drunk.

If he wasn't throwing back the liquid in the lounge, then he'd be seeking comfort and consort in his cans at the golf club. With that came the uncertainty as I lay in my bed and waited for him to return. I would lie there clutching the curtain tight in my small hand. I would pull the fabric down, almost straight, forming a strained sliver, and peer into the blackness, unblinking. It seemed I was always watching and waiting. Sometimes I searched for satellites between the twinkles of light, but mostly the fear in my tummy distracted me.

Other times I prayed.

"*Gentle Jesus, meek and mild*
Look upon a little child;

Pity mice, and little me
Suffer me to come to Thee.
Please keep my mother safe
And us.
Amen"

When the far-off beams of his car's lights finally cut through the milky curtain that draped the sky I would look straight ahead into the distance. I would see the flicker of his headlights break between the trees far away and I'd gauge how long he was taking. The longer he took the greater the certainty. Time left hanging was a broken promise of a silent night.

I would keep my eyes fixed on the beams of light as he weaved up the driveway. Only when he parked would I lose sight of his car and only then would I blink. I'd keep my ears sharp. I'd wait to see how long it took for him to open the car door. I'd wait to see how long it took for him to close the car door. I'd listen to hear how lazy the thud was. Then, ears pricked, I'd follow his stagger up the path. I knew exactly where he'd fall. Just past the flowerbed beneath the thorn tree. I'd hear him pick himself up.

I would keep my hand balanced tight on the edge of my bed as I held the curtain firm and steady. I would lie there, still and unseen, peeping out. He never made the stairs. They were right outside my window and I would draw back into the darkness as he lay prone. I would want to close my ears as he cursed, but I couldn't in case he saw the curtain move. His words were distorted and muffled as he collided with the veranda. He would roll over. I would watch him as he tried to focus. He would fix his eyes, unblinking, stare straight ahead and eventually lurch forward. Often he would crawl. Sometimes he would vomit.

My chest would tighten some more when he spewed his acid. Only then would I carefully slide my curtain closed.

But somehow he always had enough in him for the fight.

The beatings usually took place at night. They seldom happened during the day.

Except one particular Saturday afternoon when he came home early from the golf club. My mother had greeted him in her usual manner, a grand smile on her face, her placatory mask of pretence, pretending he wasn't raging drunk. But he needed no provocation. He never did.

As the thumps started, I grabbed my brother and sister and shepherded them into the TV room.

"It's going to be okay," I whispered as we cowered together.

"We'll be okay."

"I promise."

They were only seven. I was two years older. It was my job to keep them safe.

We waited for the quiet and only when my mother lay sobbing into the pillows in her room did we sneak out. We made sure my father wouldn't hear us. We made no noise, not a sound, as we squeezed ourselves between the wires of the boundary fence, carefully avoiding the sharpened barbs, to enter into the Badenhorsts' property. It was only once we were on the other side, on their land, that we dared to raise our voices. We rushed around their veld, a land dense with protea bushes. All those shrubs hanging abundant with massive woolly flowers tinted in murky shades of carmine and pink, and layers of dusty cream. We picked only the finest. We stood tall and ripped at thick, stubborn woody stems to reach for the most voluptuous, most colourful and most beautiful, growing free and wild in our neighbours' veld.

And, as we laughed and made a noise and filled our arms, we allowed ourselves to forget.

This would make my mother feel better. We knew she would be happy and smile too.

We cleared the stems of their dark green, glossy leaves and filled all the vases we could find. And when there weren't enough of those, we found jars and pressed them full. We placed them all over the dining room and lounge, infusing the house with a strong, dusty, leathery smell.

Then we waited.

She finally appeared, eyes swollen and puffy. She saw the flowers, then she took us one by one over her knee. Each word accompanied by a slap.

"YOU – WILL – NOT – STEAL –" Four syllables. Four slaps.
"EVER!" she shouted. Five.

"Take these back to Mrs Badenhorst now!" Pause. "And you say sorry for stealing her flowers."

Mrs Badenhorst seemed a little taken aback by our arrival, but courteously and unquestioningly accepted her flowers back.

It was two months later that my brother set off a firecracker and flicked a spark that would soon twist into a raging furnace that would take the Badenhorsts' veld with it. All the proteas would be destroyed, charred and blackened, yet somehow the Badenhorsts continued to welcome us into their home.

But it was then, that day, as I emptied my arms of my heavy bouquet and rubbed its downy dust away, and with tears still drying on my cheeks that I promised myself ...

This will never happen to me.
I will never be beaten up.
Never. Ever.

Seven

We met neither by accident nor by chance, nor were we introduced. We just knew each other. It was not an intuitive knowing, not some inexplicable familiarity that stretched between searching souls to vibrate deeply and divinely. It was a simple connection. I knew him through work. He was a camera operator in the film industry.

But that was a long time ago. My life had moved on.

I was no longer married to the man for whom I was going to keep the home fires burning. My career was flourishing. I was flying on the wings of good fortune, grabbing at stars as I soared past with my five-year-old son tucked tightly under the tips of my wing. I was thirty years old and focused on leveraging the updrafts. I was not floating around aimlessly. I wasn't looking to find myself, nor was I looking for anyone to whisper to my heart. Not that I didn't appreciate sweet, soft murmurings, but how would I manage it all? Twenty-four hours in a day didn't stretch long enough to be an accessible mother, to co-anchor a daily radio show, to present three television programmes and also anchor the late-night TV news – all this in between guest appearances, public events and interviews for glossy magazines. I didn't think there was a yearning cavity to be filled. In fact, if anyone had asked, I would have said there wasn't even the faintest fissure for anyone to make an entrance in my life, never mind turn on the light.

There had, though, been some who'd attempted to flick the switch.

Being on national television and the biggest commercial radio station in the country brought its own allure and over the years I was flattered to receive letters, cards and messages from viewers and listeners alike. It was not unheard of to walk out after a broadcast and find a bouquet of flowers that had been delivered to reception. I once received a set of diamond earrings but, as thrilling as it was, felt compelled to return them. There were two occasions when I requested security to physically escort two of the more ardent fans from my workplace.

One morning a large, padded envelope was waiting for me as I arrived at the studio. Enclosed was a pencil portrait of me meticulously etched and shaded by an inmate from Mangaung Maximum Security Prison. I appreciated the drawing, and still have it safely tucked away, but it was admittedly unsettling. My first thoughts had been of how the artist had held that newspaper article, with my picture on the front page, tight in his hand, or possibly alongside a heavily tattooed arm, or maybe positioned close to a shaved chest, as he frowned and focused on the intricacies and nuances of my facial features. I couldn't help but wonder why he was in a maximum-security prison. What if he was a murderer? His was an uninvited intimacy and an unnerving thought.

However, I was considerably more unnerved one morning to receive a call at the radio station from a man yet to *become* a prisoner. My headphones were clamped to my ears, my voice still raw from reading the 07:00 news bulletin. It was the lead story that was so chilling. Yet another woman had been found; dumped, viciously beaten, raped and strangled with her underwear. The murders were escalating and it was apparent that this serial killer was becoming more brazen and more violent.

I was still shuffling the pages of the bulletin when I saw the red light flashing, indicating that a call was being put through to the studio by the sound engineer. It was a call for me. The caller was softly spoken, perfectly polite, calmly and courteously requesting copies of the news items on the serial killings. I kept my voice even as I responded, explaining that all hard copies were discarded and that I wouldn't be able to assist him.

It was only after I put the phone down that I heard Tupac's 'Keep Ya Head Up' bouncing around the studio as Bob, the DJ, competed in volume with his favourite artist. Bob echoing Tupac's words, assuring us that all we had to do was keep our head up, that things were going to get easier, much brighter.

I looked over at Bob, my brow knitted tight.

He swiftly slammed his hand down on the mute button and bawled across the consul, "What?"

"I've just spoken to the serial killer," I said.

"Seriously?"

"Yip."

I tried to trace the call, but he had already disappeared, lost amid the complex circuitry of the electronic switchboard. And I had let him get away. It later transpired that he had contacted other radio stations and it had been a quick-thinking newspaper journalist who had lured him to his dramatic capture. He, Moses Sithole, was eventually convicted of thirty-eight brutal murders and sentenced to 2410 years in a maximum-security prison. No thanks to me.

It seemed our station was particularly popular among prison inmates, with a listenership almost evenly divided between us and an independent talk-radio station. It took a while for me to grasp the concept of prisoners tuning into our voices every morning, sharing our thoughts, our humour, happiness or outrage, generally being part of our conversation, as they sat alone in a bleak, barred cell, or with far too many others, sweaty and congested in an over-crowded room, sharing their morning breath, while our voices cleaved the surrounding din.

Radio listening is an intimate experience where reality and fantasy intertwine, and it's often easy for listeners to forget that presenters really are strangers. It was not uncommon for us to receive calls from inmates. There was one particular prisoner who was unwavering in his thinking that I was his friend and that I was obliged to post his bail. He called a number of times and insisted there was a *misunderstanding* about a car that he allegedly borrowed, a minor oversight that would soon be sorted out if only I'd make that payment. It was disquieting to have to convince him that I would not be the one bailing him out.

But, mostly, the public had no direct access – except, one unhurried afternoon when I was behind my computer, in my office at home, I received a call from an intrepid, and rather determined Chris. Chris, from Durban, had managed to secure my private number. He had seen me on TV. He had a friend named Rob in Port Elizabeth.

Rob had recently divorced, and Chris firmly believed that the two of us were meant to be one. Chris was quite adamant and for twenty minutes I heard various versions of, "You don't understand, I think you'll be good for each other."

Chris was not easily convinced that I wasn't interested and that Port Elizabeth was a bit far from me in Johannesburg. The conversation did not end well.

"You're making a mistake," he snapped before dropping the line.

When I got another call, this time from a viewer called Bernard, I was more easily persuaded to flick the curls from my shoulders and meet for dinner. My initial response was to turn down the invitation, but Chris's insinuation that I was unreasonable and, even worse, ungracious still prickled and Bernard's repeated "You've got nothing to lose" finally won me over. And so it was that, as the sun stroked the day with a last caress, I bravely broke into the brilliant brightness of the Hyde Park shopping centre to meet a distinguished-looking, elegantly attired, white-haired man.

"Good evening," he crooned. "I'm Bernard."

Bernard was old. Old enough to be my father.

In fact, he was older ... much older.

I held on to my smile but it was then and there that I decided to decline any further invitations, no matter how convincing. Definitely not. No more.

Then *he* called. *Him.*

I hadn't given him a moment's thought over the years and was surprised to hear his voice.

"Hullo, do you remember me?"

"Why, yes, of course I do," I replied. Graciously.

He shared how his life had evolved, how he was no longer in the film industry, how he had moved into manufacturing and that he was hoping I'd be able to assist him with a marketing plan for his product. Could I give him an hour of my time? Well, of course I could. It was hardly a sacrifice. Not that I knew anything about the making of ginger beer or of its marketing.

We met at a restaurant close to my home. It was a popular meeting place, poised along the grassy slopes of the Craighall Park valley, between properties yet to be subdivided. It was only a matter of time before the green of the neighbourhood corner would surrender to the inevitability of the invading land-use trend of rezoning to commercial property, but as we met the residential noises from the avenue below provided its own muffled tune.

He had arrived ahead of me. When he stood to welcome me, I realised that I'd forgotten how tall he was. Tall and lean. His shirt was tucked neatly into chino shorts, but being so lanky, he appeared a little ungainly, almost boyishly awkward. His sleeves were casually rolled back to reveal sinuous wrists and big hands that closed easily around mine in greeting. It was an informal and comfortable gesture. I slipped in opposite him as he settled himself back down, his broad shoulders rolling forward as he stretched his legs out loosely before him; languidly, like a wild cat, with the same fluid grace belying its strength and deadliness.

Time was equally graceful as it stalked the day. It was still early, too early for the lunchtime rush, so we sat, the two of us, alone, cradled on the deck basking in the warm glow of the midday sun. It wouldn't be long before the day would be overwhelmed by the scorching intensity of February's summer, an intensity that could only be defeated by a late-afternoon shower, but as we chatted away the air was still breathing, the trees were free of shadow and the clouds were deftly marbling the blue sky above us.

He told me how he'd read a recent article on me in *Fair Lady* magazine. Naturally, I was intrigued – not many men read glossy women's magazines, do they? Clearly I was wrong. It was a thoughtful article, well articulated and well written, that enquired about everything, from my dreams and aspirations, to my thoughts on God, my views on money, my fear of failure, to the identity of my most treasured possession.

As we sat there discussing the article, we chuckled about how I was asked: "What's the best gossip you've heard about yourself?" I had answered that Bob the DJ and my ex-husband both agreed that I was the most conservative person they knew.

And what was I looking for in a man? It was a simple response: "He shouldn't be gay, an alcoholic, a paedophile or a wife batterer. Aside from any of those – he could be anything." It was an answer that was altogether spontaneous and carefree, but regrettably, carelessly crass.

But how we laughed, the two of us, out there on that deck.

I was quite fascinated that he'd remembered all those details. I hadn't put him down as a sensitive, thoughtful man, but his questions made me feel safe, interesting and valued.

I had known him years before, from the time I was a crewing agent in the film industry and he was one of the crew. I hadn't known him well and had seldom managed any of his bookings, but I knew enough about him to know he was not considered measured in his manner. In fact, he had a reputation for being abrasive and prone to aggressive outbursts.

But as I watched him throw back his head and laugh, I was captivated by his charm and I berated myself, thinking how easily and unquestioningly I had accepted those judgements of him. As I sat there, caught in the autumn of his gaze, I saw him differently, a handsome man, rugged but gentle. His eyes were brown, dry oak leaves. They were sharp and keen, rustling with intelligence. His movements were expansive, and I liked the way he gesticulated with his arms as he talked, how he flicked his wrists like a tiger flicks its tail before it leaps. And his hands ... they were beautiful. They were working hands. A little rough and calloused, browned from too much sun. I looked at my hands holding a glass of dry white. They were so much smaller, and paler. My nails were newly polished into a soft, pink glow.

I glanced around to see that we were no longer alone. The tables around us had filled with other diners, mostly men on their lunch-hour break. They had ordered freshly tapped beers and were smoking and their laughter and loud talk peppered the air. Waiters blended in seamlessly as they glided past us carrying armfuls of chargrilled steaks sizzling on heated cast-iron bases, trailing smoky wisps of barbecue and cooked herbs.

The ice that clinked lightly in our glasses soon melted as our lunchtime meeting stretched beyond midday and the late-afternoon shadows dappled the deck. When we eventually parted, having established much earlier that I wasn't going to be an effective link in his marketing strategy, he casually tossed over his shoulder, "Can I phone you sometime?"

"Sure," I laughed, making my way to the car, my steps light like a cat high-stepping as it pranced down a bright alley.

Eight

It was never a formal courtship. Not some masterful seduction. Perhaps I should have demanded more. Perhaps I should have asked more questions. Where had he been staying before? Who had he been staying with? Why had he suddenly appeared in my life? But I never did. Or if I did, there wasn't much to his answers. I never knew where he came from, just as one day I wouldn't know where he went.

But back then it was a comfortable and gradual progression of an unexpected relationship. To me it all seemed so fortuitous, that he was a heart-stopping detour in my strategically managed life. As time passed and I got to know him better, I was to understand how *misunderstood* this wonderful man was.

He told me of his youth, of his family's blue-chip social circle and the many different exclusive schools. He spoke of new cricket bats being delivered to the sports field by chauffeurs driving a showcase of the finest in motoring excellence. It was a life that pulsed with privilege.

But there is nothing in this life that does not cast a shadow.

He spoke of sitting alone on the back seat of those stately cars, a little boy all on his own, his father always working, his mother in a darkened room behind a closed door. His father, by all accounts, a successful man, driven and selfish, but with a deep-seated complex about his compromised height and, as with some who spend their entire lives looking up at others, he overcompensated by ruthlessly seeking power and conquest. And, with her six-foot stature, his mother became a daily reminder of his father's physical shortcomings. She, in turn, sounded lost, as though she'd withdrawn into herself at some sad point, an alcoholic, who loathed her husband and who neglected her children.

That's what he told me. And that's what I believed.

I shook off my discomfort when I heard how he and his brother had sued his mother for their inheritance. I'd never heard of such a thing before. Perhaps it had been necessary, I reassured myself. I knew how much we ourselves had lost because of my father's all-consuming need for yet another drink. I knew the devastation of careless financial ruin. Perhaps she had been incapable of managing the family finances. Perhaps. Maybe.

He told me of his ex-girlfriend. She was crazy. Completely irrational and insane. It seemed that they were always fighting. I overheard a conversation between them once. I heard his phone ring. It was her. He moved discreetly off, but not beyond earshot. I could hear him.

He was rattled by the call. It unsettled him. Disturbed him.

He stalked up and down the passage, his voice booming as he shouted her down with his final words, "Leave me alone, you fucking bitch."

Afterwards, when he strode into the kitchen, his eyes still flashing in fury, his lips thin and tight, he gave pause, shrugged his shoulders, and stilled. I breathed in long and deep.

"You wouldn't speak to me like that, would you," I said. It wasn't a question.

"I'd never do that to you," he said. "You'd never deserve it."

No, I'd never deserve it. He was right.

Then he grinned.

She really must be insane, I thought.

We spoke of loss and longing and love.

I had recently lost my father, but he knew that already – it was in the *Fair Lady* piece. I had been asked when last I had cried and I had spoken of my father dying the week before the interview. And I had cried. Not a deluge of tears that flooded my being from a deep and devastating, mind-numbing loss – I would never feel that sense of bereavement for my father. I hadn't seen him for the last five years of his life. I heard that he had been found dead on the floor by some local fishermen. They were his friends apparently. He was fifty-two years old. After his death I saw the picture on his ID and he looked much, much older than that. He looked at least eighty. All colour seemed to have drained from him. His face was ashen, his forehead furrowed, cheeks carved with thick grooves. But what really made him look aged was the madness in his eyes.

I don't know what he died of. I don't know the specifics. I suspect his body was simply exhausted from the years of abuse.

But what I do know is that I gave up on him long before his body did.

And yet, although I would never be swamped in sorrow at his passing, I did cry. I cried tears of sadness. I was sad that I never had the father I wanted or needed. Sad that I would never know him as a man with dreams, hopes and aspirations for a greater tomorrow. Sad that his alcoholism had denied me the opportunity of knowing him as much else other than a tortured, broken, mean-spirited, angry and violent man. I do have some memories of him being different, from when I was a child. They are vague and fuzzy, though, and I've had to think hard.

I remember that he used to allow me to sit on his lap as he drove the car up the gravel road and I breathed in the musk of his Old Spice aftershave. I remember that I used to drive the tractor with him, or run alongside, as he ploughed the fields for hours and how the sun burnt the back of his neck and the top of his bald head.

I recall how he loved showing 35-millimetre movies, and how he'd line the projector up on a stack of books for a Sunday-night viewing, moving up and down in front of the tunnel of light, making sure that he got it just right, casting a long shadow across the lounge wall, the projector clicking and whirring loudly as we waited.

That he loved to cook. And bake. Especially curries and meat pies – he particularly enjoyed making those – and I was usually his assistant and had to peel the potatoes and cut the onions. He left me that, his love of making food.

I remember, too, how his shoulders would shake as he laughed. And how his eyes watered.

I remember that I was his favourite.

But that was a lifetime ago.

The last time I'd really looked at my father – properly looked at him – he was crying. It was the last time we had all been together as a family. My mother was sitting, holding my much younger brother. My sister and I sat alongside her – we were on one side, my father on the other. My brother, David, was lying in a coffin between us.

It was the first time we'd been together in a room for many years and we'd never be together again.

Then I was defeated by death.

When I lost my brother I lost myself. I had wanted it to be me. Why him?

I had fought so hard to keep him safe. But that weekend he was still in the army and he was coming home for his final pass when he took the Olifantsfontein bend at speed, lost control of his vehicle and died. I had tried to protect him, even at the very end, when I tried to get him out of Angola where he had been based for his military service.

He was in the technical services retrieval division, his job to silently creep through the bush, under the protection of darkness, and enter the war zone to retrieve broken-down trucks and vehicles. He was in a foreign country, alone, for days at a time, his face greased and his body camouflaged in dirt. He was exhausted by all the violence. He was afraid. One day he'd phoned me from a payphone at the army base.

"You need to help me," he'd said, his voice deep and hoarse.

"You need to get me outta here." There was a brief silence.

"If you don't …" His words choked. "I'm not going to make it."

I knew he was crying.

David, six foot three, with shoulders like a Brahman bull, was falling apart on the other end of the line. He was begging me to help him. This was my brother, the one afraid of so little. It was he who would fearlessly rush up the stairs to find me on the dance floor at the Molani Hotel in Brits, the light bouncing off the mirror ball. I'd see him on the other side, across from the bar where watered-down double brandy and Cokes were poured generously. He'd be beckoning me from the other side, his arms waving wildly.

"Tracy, come quickly," his voice raised in excitement. "Come watch. I'm going to fight."

And I would be right behind him, shouting for him to be careful, knowing that I couldn't stop him, but all the time hoping it would be over by the time the cops arrived and that there'd be no need for an ambulance. The dance floor emptying behind me as everyone pushed their way outside.

"*Kom gou. Hulle gaan baklei.*"

"*Dis die Engelsman.*"

"*Hulle gaan mekaar bliksem.*"

"*Watch. Nou kom 'n lekker snotklap.*"

But now my brother was feeling hopeless. The boy who would steal his father's beers and take them back to boarding school with him on a Sunday night, where under the hooded veil of darkness he and his friends would knock them back, hiding beneath the unlit stairs, pushing to see if he'd be caught. David, the one was always looking for more.

Now he wasn't coping.

Hearing his words reminded me instantly of a time years before when I'd been woken by a lion. A lion roaring flames of fire. A dream. Just a dream. There was no need for me to search for an underlying meaning. It had come to me instantly. I knew that my brother must never go to the army or he would die. The lion would swallow him in its fiery jaws.

I rushed into the kitchen at breakfast the next morning,

"Mom, whatever you do, you mustn't let David go to the army," I pleaded. "I had a dream ... Please, Mom."

"Yes," she had said, nodding her head vigorously in an attempt to reassure me that she was taking me seriously. My brother was ten years old.

A decade later he made that call.

"What do you want me to do?" I asked.

"Get me out."

"I'll do what I can," I said. "I promise."

And I did. I picked up the telephone directory and looked up the contact details of the office of General Magnus Malan, Minister of Defence. I asked to speak to him. His secretary told me that he was unavailable but she kindly put me onto the brigadier general's office. Astonishingly, the brigadier general agreed to meet with me.

A few days later I was guided through the security checkpoint in my rattling 140Y Datsun onto the army base in Pretoria. In the parking lot I was met by a young uniformed man, not much younger than my twenty-one years. He escorted me through the military maze to the brigadier general's office. The brigadier general did not keep me waiting. When his secretary ushered me in, he stood tall behind his desk and then stepped forward to greet me. His insignia was polished bright on his epaulette, bronze on maroon. I sat down opposite him at his desk, and stretched myself straight, straighter than the old South African flag hanging in the corner and fast losing its lustre. It was only once my heels were anchored before me, my ankles touching and my skirt tucked neatly around my knees that I told him of the promise I had made to my brother.

He summoned the Army chaplain and so it was that the three of us sat together and discussed the matter further over a cup of tea. We chatted as we nibbled on dry-baked biscuits and sipped from the finest Royal Albert china served off a polished sterling-silver tray. It was an unhurried gathering and I left the base assured in the knowledge that the South African government and the Defence Force were pulling all their forces out of Angola. The war was finally over. I also had their personal undertaking that my brother's departure would be expedited.

It wasn't.

He was among the very last troops to be withdrawn from the Angolan border.

And he had only two weeks left in the army when he recklessly took that hairpin bend at speed, lost control, and was flung from the vehicle, tossed aside and discarded, a maimed soldier who had lost his last battle. He had been lying broken and dying along the verge for hours before the emergency medical services arrived. But by then it was too late; he'd taken his last shallow breath and could no longer be resuscitated. So, instead, the ambulance personnel removed his still body from the scene and then callously helped themselves to all his personal belongings, taking the shoes and clothes I'd bought him the last time I had seen him.

My brother died with his hand on the steering wheel. There was no other vehicle involved. It was him, the turn, and the accelerator beneath his foot, ensnaring him, luring him, drawing him in to the fiery mouth of the roaring lion.

He was wild and angry, and constantly needed to challenge the world around him in his desperate attempt to make sense of it, but he was also the young man who took his father's gun apart, separating the bolt from the barrel, to keep his mother safe in his own absence. He took the mechanism with him and stowed it like a silent secret in the back of his school locker.

While my brother might have courted danger in life, in death his parting was dignified and precise. When he died, he was a young man in uniform, which meant he was entitled to a military funeral. It was an honourable farewell where his comrades-in-arms stood as one and raised their right hands to their berets in a last goodbye before his flag-draped coffin was loaded into the hearse and he made his final journey away from us.

As the long, black vehicle drove off, I wanted to follow.

I wanted to shout and scream and rip the clothes from my body.

My brother was dead.

He was gone.

I felt as though my soul had been syphoned from my body, that the air within me was gone, senselessly stolen from within me.

I saw my father once more after that final salute.

My son was six months old and perhaps it was the endless cycle of life, death and birth that drew me to him. I wanted to introduce my child to his grandfather. My father had been living quietly in his mother's garden cottage for many years when we visited. But we didn't stay long. My father had lost his sense of being and, it seems, large chunks of his mind too. He spoke impressively of his plans and what he was doing. But none of it was true. He had long ago succumbed to the fanciful flights of his mind. He was unwashed, dirty; he rambled incoherently and my son screamed every time his grandfather came near him. I never saw or spoke to him again.

But, still, I was sad to bury my father.

○

We had that in common, he and I. He had lost both his parents. We could talk about it. He understood.

It seemed as though the gods of fortune had sacrificed their souls for me. Besides the ampleness they had already bestowed on me – my son, my career – they had now delivered me a soul mate. A good man with whom I could share my life.

This was clearly going to be a journey of mutual discovery, of support and understanding. I was overwhelmed, not only because we had such a strong personal connection, but also because we were both so focused on our futures. He had recently bought a fledgling ginger-beer bottling company with his inheritance. I was building my career. He was fascinated by current affairs and worked his way through the daily newspapers every morning. I was a news anchor, in negotiation with the public broadcaster to become the prime-time evening newsreader. It seemed we both demanded the most from life and were working hard to realise our dreams. We shared the same humour and I couldn't remember when last I'd enjoyed someone else's company so much. He was an answer to a question I hadn't even asked.

And I wanted to share him with everyone.

So I did.

I introduced him to my son. I introduced him to my family. I introduced him to my closest friends. I even introduced him to my ex-husband.

He, in turn, introduced me to no one. Not one single person. In all the time we were together I never met a sibling, a friend or a business acquaintance. No one.

When I asked why I had never met anyone, he explained it so easily: "I just want to be with you."

I was flattered.

I was not to be distracted.

I was a woman falling in love.

Besides, it suited me. Presenting a breakfast show brought its own limitations on my time; my days were long, my nights short.

So, in the beginning, he would make his way over in the evening for a chat and a laugh. Other evenings, he wouldn't. Sometimes I wouldn't see him for a few days. I had no idea where he lived, but he assured me it was unimportant and that he preferred being at my place. It was convenient and practical. Besides, I couldn't really press for more information as he had yet to make any promises.

So he'd disappear for a few days ... and then he'd be back.

We'd go out for dinner or settle in for a quiet evening twirling a glass of wine on my veranda.

It was all so gradual and casual and wonderful.

The first night he stayed over just happened. It is hardly worth mentioning; he was tired, it was late, and he suggested staying right where he was on my couch. And he did. It made sense.

The next night was the same.

And the next.

That was how he slipped into my life.

Straight through the front door.

And he arrived without even a suitcase.

Nine

"You're just like my mother, you fucking bitch," he snarled.

Me?

Like his mother?

No, not me.

"I'm so sorry," I said. "So, so sorry …"

But he never heard me. He was gone.

My intention had never been to hurt him. I'd been mulling my words mindfully for a while, rolling them round, trying to find the most pleasant way to present my poison. I wanted him to move out. We had never agreed to him moving in. In fact, it had never even been discussed. It didn't suit me. I had a son, after all. He also had yet to offer anything toward his board and lodging, and it had been about two months.

Our conversation had not gone well. I hadn't expected it to, but I hadn't anticipated him being quite so wounded. How could I have hurt him so?

I was so sorry.

So dreadfully sorry.

Was I really like his mother?

That was a terrible thought.

I set my pots aside and switched off the stove. I leaned in to the counter and held it tight as his rage choked me and his words ricocheted around in my head. We'd never fought like this before. A few weeks earlier he'd been upset, yes, but nothing like this.

Then he'd taken me away. It was the first time we had been truly alone. My son was with his father and the two of us were off to Mpumalanga for a dreamy getaway weekend. We'd left at midday to avoid the Friday rush-hour traffic, which meant it hadn't taken long for Johannesburg, with its gold and dust, to disappear behind us and for the landscape to change from dusty, dry and brittle to soft and gentle once we'd passed the mines of Ogies and Witbank. As the afternoon touched the tar, the road ahead became silky and flat and empty. It was just the two of us, alone, in his red Alfa Romeo.

By the time we turned off onto a rutted road and slipped into the green, the sun had draped itself over the day and fused itself to become one with the warmed earth. To our left were litchi trees deceiving us in their dormancy. And to our right, orchards of macadamias giving permission for the last of the day's rays to filter through the density of whorled leaves. Further away, avocado trees were ready to drop their swollen fruits. The land was generously offering its abundance, rich in texture and taste.

We arrived at a manor house that was a protraction of this plenitude. It was all so luxurious and opulent and lovely. Our suite, with its fine furniture, overlooked a shaded, cobbled courtyard, but we had rushed inside and barely given it a glance as we tossed our bags down and made our way back to reception to enjoy the last warm glimmer of the day. We settled ourselves down on the pillared veranda and ordered our drinks: a single-malt whiskey for him, a glass of chilled Sauvignon Blanc for me.

Dinner was an elegant and intimate affair. The small restaurant was full, light music teasing the evening air. We were seated at a small table draped in white cotton slightly rough to the touch. The heavy silver cutlery sparkled in the dimmed light and a candle flickered between us. The evening was ours.

He selected a bottle of red. The sommelier half-filled our glasses and then surreptitiously slipped away before I lifted my eyes to him, and smiled.

He didn't.

His eyes had lost their warm brown hue. They were icy as they drilled into mine.

I instantly felt their chill.

"I can't do this!" he spat.

"What's *this*?" I asked, my voice thin.

"This. Us. I can't do it," he said. "It's too much!" He heaved himself up, throwing back his chair.

Then he was gone.

He was not coming back, that much was obvious.

It's too much.

What did he mean?

I lowered my eyes and stared into my glass of wine. It seemed the contents had flushed to a deep, scarlet red. Swirling, staring back at me accusingly like blood on white cotton. As my shame washed over me I finally found the courage to lift my hand.

There was no need to summon the waiter. He was already there.

"Please bring me the bill," I asked softly.

Eyes down, I looked at no one as I scurried out.

I needed to move quickly. I had to catch him.

What if he'd left and gone back to Johannesburg?

How would I get back?

I felt the bile scaling my throat as I quickened my step. It was bitter and sour and I wanted to be sick.

Was his car still there?

It was.

I lay my hand on the bonnet. It was cold to the touch.

I quickly made my way to where our suite took form ahead. It was in darkness. The light from the courtyard strained through the entrance, but it was enough to see that the door to the room upstairs was closed. I entered cautiously, without a sound, and turned into the bedroom downstairs. The room where we'd blithely tossed our luggage a few hours earlier. His bag was gone. My shiny, black suitcase was still on the bed. Small and compact. Now sitting large and weighted full of empty promise. Packed and unpacked.

I lifted it and quietly set it alongside the open door, ready for a hasty departure.

I collapsed onto the bed and leaned back into the headboard as my thoughts tumbled around me.

What had just happened?

God forbid.

I found the corner of the sheet and starting rubbing its sharpness between my thumb and forefinger the way I used to when I was a child. Slowly. Backwards and forwards. Trying to smooth away the gnawing hollowness.

I knew it well.

It was fear.

And it took me back.

◯

We are away on holiday. I am ten years old.

Holidays were a luxury and they usually only happened once a year when my mother packed our car full of Christmas presents, home-grown pumpkins and other seasonal vegetables and we made our way to our grandmother in the Eastern Cape.

But this time it's different. It is not December, nor are we heading south.

We are going someplace else.

We are off to the land of the rising sun and the Zulu kingdom. To Durban. To see the sea, the sand and the dolphins. We'd never been there before and we'd been counting the sleeps for weeks.

I know we are only allowed one small bag each so I sort and sift my clothing with much attention to probability and any unforeseen possibility. Anything that can't fit in, I'd wear. I'd then disrobe once we were already on the journey and it was too late for my father to do anything about it.

We leave early in the morning, with me layered in masterful deceit. I'm wearing a dress and fitted snugly beneath it is a pair of jeans. Over my dress are two T-shirts, a jersey and a jacket. My discomfort is not a burden. I also intend adding to my layers as soon as we reach Durban and have brought along my savings, my birthday and pocket money, tucked away safely in my handbag on my lap. Brits is not a haven for high fashion after all.

We arrive in Durban mid-afternoon.

It is hot. A different kind of hot from the one we are used to in Brits. The air hangs thick with moisture. It is a wet that dampens and frizzes my hair as soon as my father opens the window to breathe out the burn of his congratulatory cigarette. He deserves it. He's been driving for hours and he's finally got us there safely. I watch as the thread of nicotine floats out and dances through the sea air, wickedly mimicking us on the back seat as we strain to see who will be the first to see the ocean.

It has taken a while to get to where we are staying. My father has driven up and down the endless one-ways in an attempt to find his way. But it really doesn't matter if we get a little lost along the way. It's all part of the journey and, anyway, it's thrilling to see street names we'd only ever seen on the Monopoly board.

It turns out our block of flats is not along the beachfront. It's a few roads back and we can't really see the sea, except if we stretch ourselves tall and thin and peer out on our toes. Then there it is: the sea with its waves rolling over in the distance, foaming at the edges and frothing our names, lapping at the beach, meeting the golden sand as it melts beneath the hot sun like warm hazelnut fudge.

"We're coming," I want to shout. "We'll be there now, but my mom first needs to get organised."

Our flat itself is rather drab, all a bit dark and rather unexciting but, as my mother cheerfully says, "We're only sleeping here."

And sleep is the last thing we want to do right now.

When my father circles the building in an attempt to find parking I notice some shops and immediately start to nag my sister to accompany me on my spending spree while my mother unpacks our bags and sorts the kitchen. Soon we are rushing downstairs and hopping along the pavement. We have memorised the address and promise my mother that we won't go far and won't get lost.

We're already one block down before we find the first clothing shop. It's a small boutique. I am too young to know I should be intimidated and proudly explain to the glamorous shop assistant that I am spending my birthday money. And she honours my determination by presenting me with the most beautiful dress I've ever seen. It is crisp white and gathered ever so slightly along the neckline into thin straps that tie on the shoulders. It falls well below my knees with a neat ruffle. Truth be told, it doesn't quite fit but I know I'll grow into it. I also buy my first pair of high heels. They are canvas on wedges, red-and-white stripes with rope straps that cross up my skinny calves. I have never owned an outfit so splendid before. A white, summery dress with red-and-white striped high heels. It is magnificent.

I even have enough money over to buy a necklace. There is nothing in my price range that coordinates with my beautiful new outfit, but as I riffle through the trinkets I find a fine gold-plated coil that nestles on my collarbones. It is perfectly round, with a silk flower as its centre. It is peach in colour, each petal beautifully crafted, delicate and shiny. I am not at all concerned that it doesn't all match and work together as one outfit because as the sales lady explains I can then mix and match.

We bound back, me with my empty purse and swinging my purchase proudly. Once back in the building, my sister and I agree to race each other to our flat on the third floor.

I'll take the lift. She'll scale the stairs.

On a count of three, we take off. I am determined to beat her. I laugh as I encourage the lift upwards and squeeze my way out through the lift doors before they even open properly. But she isn't there to greet me. Instead, I hear her fearful shouting from the floor below. She is screaming for my mother.

My sister had been making her way up, two stairs at a time, when she had turned the corner and run right into my father. He had been creeping along, tiptoeing down those darkened stairs like an amateur thief. Making his way home. Leaving us behind.

I fall down the stairs to get there. My mother and brother come rushing from the flat. We stand there in disbelief, suspended between the first and second floor, my mother, me, my brother and my sister, watching my father, knowing what he is capable of. This is our father, a man who could rip a birthday cake from the heart of a heated oven and deliberately toss it away, flinging it out the kitchen door in a grand gesture of command, reminding us of who has the power, leaving us with only the faintest essence of vanilla.

"Where are you going?" my mother asks.

"Home."

I think I see the shame in his eyes. Not the shame for a pitiful act. The shame at having been caught. Then he lifts his chin as he looks at each of us, one at a time, deliberate and defiant.

If I hadn't been looking at him I would have missed it. It is the briefest flicker of pleasure, a fleeting flash of fulfilment. He is pleased. He is delighted with our disappointment and our fear.

There is nowhere to go but back.

It is the end of our holiday in Durban.

☉

So as I lay against the headboard, I knew not to be left behind. I knew not to settle down into the duck-down duvet and succumb to the night. I knew to keep vigil.

I heard him making his way down the stairs in the morning.

"I'm leaving now," he muttered as he passed my door.

I scuttled after him.

For the four hours back to Johannesburg, we never spoke once, not a word. We sat together in our disconnect of silence, with me trying to work out where it had gone wrong.

I blamed myself.

He was clearly feeling trapped and pressured and I had made him feel that way.

He dropped me back at home and then left. I never knew where. It was a few days before I saw him again, but it was a long time before I'd realise that it wasn't me he wanted to get away from. There had been something he wanted to get to. And it had been a far greater force than my presence. But, sitting in stony silence on that seemingly endless journey back from Mpumalanga, I had thought it was my fault.

As I stood breathing deep and holding onto my kitchen counter a few weeks later, I knew it was my fault. It was me who had asked him to move out and he had taken it as soul-crushing rejection. What was wrong with me? Why did I say I was uncomfortable supporting him financially? I should have handled it differently.

My heart lifted when fifteen minutes later he was striding down my passage.

"Here!" he said, his eyes narrowed. "It's obviously important to you."

His words cut to the bone as fifty-rand notes fanned out over my kitchen counter.

What could I say?

I'm so sorry.

Please stay.

Ten

"You've told everyone I'm a drug addict," he said, tightening his grip on my arm.

Of course I hadn't.

It was the last thing I'd want anyone to know. Especially not my work colleagues.

Was he insane?

And if I had wanted them to know, this certainly wasn't the place I'd tell them.

We were at Insomnia nightclub in Illovo for the launch of Janet Jackson's album *The Velvet Rope*. I had been invited as a familiar voice and a famous face, and all around me were other equally, if not far more, familiar voices and famous faces. We mingled among important radio execs, hip music producers, talented musicians, society columnists, cool journalists, trendy A&R managers and young record company reps. The place was literally glittering with local stars. Everyone trying to hear each other above the drum of the music as they threw back free drinks, bounced to the beat, bumped into each other and laughed out loud. It was a grand event and it was good to be there. I was with my people and he was there as my partner.

Amid the deafening noise and pulsating strobe lights, the deeper meaning of Janet Jackson's album totally slipped me by.

I was oblivious that the title of the album, *The Velvet Rope*, was a metaphor for her own emotional boundaries. I didn't know she was singing herself naked, about her own life, introspecting on everything from her own depression to her fractured self-image as a victim of domestic violence. In fact, I barely noticed the video images magnified on the large screens all around the venue. They were just a visual backdrop to an awesome party.

All that changed when his voice slashed the smoky air.

Then I was suddenly aware of everything, even Janet Jackson as she cut across the rhythm to the chorus and sang her truth of darker themes.

"We're going," he said, yanking my arm and half dragging me from the venue.

By the time we reached the parking lot my car keys were firmly in his hand.

"You're not driving," I said. "It's my car and you've been drinking."

It was hard to focus, to keep my car on the road, with him rocking backwards and forwards into my face, spewing his sewage. He was like a madman on a runaway horse, howling, flailing his arms. His eyes were wide, frozen open like bottomless pits of black dead. He kept gripping his head and dragging his fingers through his hair. He was laughing like a lunatic when he reached in close and jerked at the handbrake, yanking it up hard, tearing it from its socket. I screamed as the rear wheels locked and we spun out of control. We were spinning straight into the traffic. Then, as the car jerked to a shuddering stop, I opened the door. As I leapt out, he lashed out and grabbed at me, ripping my sleeve. I stumbled. Two cars stopped. He was shouting at them and then at me.

"Are you okay?" one driver yelled.

I was unsure what to do.

I was standing in the middle of the road, my sleeve torn from my jacket, and five terrifying metres away were my car keys in the ignition, with my house keys attached.

It seemed there was no other way.

"I'll be fine," I said to the driver. "Thank you."

By the time I got back to the car, I was shaking.

Now *he* was behind the steering wheel.

My fingers were icy as I gripped the edge of my seat and he flattened his foot on the accelerator, flying down First Avenue West. I screamed as he shot stop streets and cleaved pavements, and then slammed on brakes just millimetres from garden walls, stalling, reversing, lurching forward again, then picking up speed, his voice filling my car, his words reverberating in my head: "I'm going to fucking kill you."

I was still crying and pleading when he opened my garage door and accelerated into the concrete columns of my garage, screaming, "Tonight you're going to die."

As the columns collapsed and the front of my car crumpled, I bolted, screaming, down the road, but he caught me by my hair and hauled me back, into my house. He locked the front door, unplugged the landline and took my cellphone apart. Then he dragged me down the passage to my room. It was there that he held me captive through the night. Him and me. He the raving, frothing captor; me the captive, the hostage.

"If a word of this comes out you're dead," he said, running his hand across his throat, his fingers gliding across his neck like a sharp knife through ribbon. "And you have a child … six months, one year … I've got time," he said, winking, reinforcing his threat.

"You know you're pathetic," he shouted.

"Yes," I said.

"You know you're nothing."

"Yes, I know."

"You know I can kill you right now, you cunt," he hissed, his hands hard around my throat.

"Yes, I know," I said, the words hoarse and dry.

"Say sorry, you bitch."

"Sorry."

"I always wanted to fuck a TV presenter … and you weren't worth it."

There was no end.

As I lay pinned to my bed with him looming above me, and as the torment continued relentlessly, it all started falling into place. At the launch, we'd been sitting with a former national soccer star turned radio and TV commentator when he'd seen someone he knew. It had been so sudden that I hardly noticed him disappear into the throng. I'd glanced up to see him greeting a man I'd never seen before. They shook hands. They grinned. They patted each other on the shoulder. They seemed delighted to see each other. Then the lights strobed and they were in darkness. I looked away. He was gone only a short while. And when he returned he was someone else.

I had fallen hard for the other man, the smart, funny, creative, talented one. Not the one with the mouth of a sailor, sordid and sour. The one who took my son to harvest fresh mussels off the rocks and carefully cleaned them of their grit, sand and debris. The one who bought books about birds and pointed them out to my boy as they fluttered by. And flew paper jets with him too. But that one was no more. Had he even existed?

It had taken a while for me to put the bleak picture together.

In the beginning I had been completely unaware. If I didn't see him for a few days, I never questioned it. If he came and went, I accepted it and actually valued it as a delightful detail to an unhurried courtship. But when he moved into my home, I soon became very aware of his flipside, his behaviour increasingly odd and erratic. The stories became more bizarre. Burglaries at work, his phone switched off, gone for a day or two at a time. I started suspecting. I started asking questions.

"I don't do fucking narcotics," he said.

But I wasn't so sure.

"I'll be home now," he said late one afternoon. But he wasn't.

By midnight I had visions of him lying alone in a gutter, overdosed, desperate or dead. The next day I trawled the streets trying to find him. I didn't know where to look. I didn't know anyone in his life. I had never met them. But still I tried to find him.

It was another two days before he loped through the front door, his head hanging low. He bled out his story. Yes, he was an addict. It had been a momentary and regrettable relapse. He was a broken man. He needed me.

Please, another chance.

We had been together for five months and I had been prepared to give it more. I was prepared to give it another chance.

Now I was going to die. Here, a hostage in my own bedroom.

I didn't want to die.

So I did all I could to stay alive.

I wrote the letter he made me write. I wrote it word for word as he throttled it out of me, as he dictated it, me *admitting* to my insanity and apologising for having accused him of being a drug addict.

I struggled silently against his grip each time he wrenched my fingers from my wrought-iron bedpost and dragged me across the bedroom. I knew to anchor myself, push myself down, my heels scuffing the polished parquet floor in protest, knowing that if he got me back to my car he would drive me to my death.

I put my knuckles to my mouth and was quiet when he stalked up and down the passage, his eyes burning, his breath hot, stabbing repeatedly at his phone calling the *Sunday Times* night desk, then *The Star*, threatening to destroy me.

"I have money. I have power. You have nothing. *Nothing!*" he screamed.

I looked at him when told to, but mostly I looked down – and that was when I prayed ... *Please God, don't let him kill me.*

I agreed with him, nodded and apologised.

I spoke, supplicated and was silent.

I stayed awake.

I didn't sleep.

I did all I could not to die.

By the time the sun was up and its cold light trickled weakly in from the north, he was exhausted. It had been nine and a half hours and he was spent.

I heard him on his phone in the lounge, calling someone to fetch him.

It was hard to believe it was over.

But when I heard my dog, Garp, whelp in pain I knew he would finally be gone.

"Get out of my fucking way," he snarled as the front door slammed behind him.

Eleven

"Sorry, my girl, but there's nothing much I can do."

"But you have to do *something*, Dad!" I wail.

"What? What can I do?" he shrugs, dragging the limp body of the dog across the tar and off the road.

He leaves it there. Dying. As if that's what one does.

Perhaps, many years later, my father would feel some of that pain, the ache of losing a beloved companion, when he found his own border collie floating in a lagoon with a brick tied to its neck. Maybe he would remember when, with dulled reflexes, he had been too slow to avoid the collision. Maybe he would hear it again: the thud, the dying whimpers. Maybe he would think of a child, of a family that lost its dog. Maybe not.

His breath, fusty with beer and tobacco, touches me as he leans forward and shuttles into first gear. It lingers over me like lukewarm death.

"Let's go," he says cheerfully, giving me a conspiratorial wink.

I turn away. I refuse to let him see my tears, drops of despair, as he accelerates past the butchery, past the panel beater, past PPC Cement, under the bridge, into Pretoria.

My father is taking me back to boarding school. I am thirteen years old.

There was no English high school in Brits so we scattered

ourselves between Rustenburg, Potchefstroom and Pretoria. I had chosen an all-girls' school in Pretoria. It was a magnificent institution, one with a fine reputation, but I had not been guaranteed automatic access. I had needed to apply.

My interview had been anticipated for a while. I had been excused from school for the day and, as the sun brought its promise from the east, I had sat there, poised before my mirror, steadying my excited and anxious thoughts. I had selected my best-fitting school dress the night before and was dressed and almost ready for breakfast. I was ironing my curls with my hands when my father's words serrated the warm, buttery air and flattened the sizzle of eggs being fried in the kitchen.

"She will not be going!"

The morning sun plunged through the sky. My hands stilled.

I heard my mother set the frying pan aside and ask innocuously, "What do you mean? Why?"

"She's not going!" he said again. "Why? *Why?*" he sneered. "Because I said so, that's why."

I was well aware of my father's meanness, knew it all too well, but still I was taken aback. We had been talking, planning and plotting this interview for months.

What now?

I listened.

"She will be going," said my mother, deliberately placing the frying pan back onto the stove.

It was the first time I had heard her defy him. It was a bold defiance. And as the air once again swelled with heated butter, its acrid aftertaste already burnt my tongue. I knew, like with any contemptuous act of disrespect, that there would be consequences.

After breakfast my mother and I made our way to Pretoria, mulling over possible questions and answers to my impending interview. The headmistress, Miss Mullins, was reputed to be formidable, as formidable in height as she was in presence. And as she opened the door it was her feet that I saw first. They were huge. They were long and narrow, encased in shoes I had only seen the Queen wear.

And I knew what shoes the Queen wore as she'd featured in

many a tale over family lunches. My aunt, Margaret, had been chosen to present King George VI's wife, Queen Elizabeth, with flowers during their royal visit to Bechuanaland (now Botswana) in 1947. This oft-repeated story left me with a visual of my aunt, a seven-year-old slip of a thing, leaning over royal shoes as she offered her delicate bouquet.

Many years later I would receive a gold-embossed calling card from the Master of the Household commanding my presence at a reception in Durban, at the Royal Hotel, to meet with Queen Elizabeth II and the Duke of Edinburgh. It was a splendid and intimate affair with only about thirty invited guests so I got to see those handcrafted, calf-leather shoes with my very own eyes.

The Queen presented often in my childhood memories. As the story went, my grandparents were once invited to Buckingham Palace so that my grandfather could be presented with a CBE, Commander of the Most Excellent Order of the British Empire, for his service to the Empire. My grandmother had scoffed at the thought of having tea with the Queen in her palace. I remembered her words clearly.

"For goodness' sake," she'd said, "who has time for tea!"

My grandmother was also a headmistress but I never saw her wearing queenly shoes.

I tried not to stare at Miss Mullins as I folded my neck backwards to look into a face that seemed awfully far away. Her blue-rinse was lacquered high and added to her steepness. I had never seen a woman so tall, nor so chillingly elegant. Her welcome, however, was warm and her greeting gracious. But as I trailed her lingering rose scent I was relieved not to be seated in the plush armchairs that demanded attention as you entered, majestic and stately in their flushed floral. It was easier to be polite, and sit tall and not swing my legs, as my hands rubbed at the cushion of the carved hardback chair. My mother was enthroned alongside me. She too was sitting tall, straight and polite.

I had been forewarned to mesmerise Miss Mullins with my brilliance and to sound intelligent. I had arrived armed with invaluable information from those who'd gone before me.

According to rampant rumour, the headmistress was not impressed with either the Nancy Drew or the Hardy Boys series as a choice of literature, preferring something a little more erudite. It was also reported that she had little tolerance for the frivolity of the Arts.

"So what type of books do you enjoy reading?" she asked, leaning forward from behind the biggest desk I'd ever seen.

"Nancy Drew and the Hardy Boys," I said.

"Aah ... And what would you like to be when you grow up?"

"An actress," I mumbled.

"Mmm ... And what sport do you prefer?"

"Athletics."

"We don't run here. Ladies never run."

Oh no. This was not going well. At all.

But I couldn't lie.

There was no need to glance sideways at my mother to know that her eyes were blazing bright, her cheeks rounded, rigid with forced radiance, giving me that *now-is-not-the-time-to-let-me-down* smile. I preferred not to see her disappointment, so instead I stared straight ahead at Miss Mullins.

Once my interview was over my mother requested that she and Miss Mullins speak privately. Outside her office there was nowhere to sit so I settled myself down on the stairs and tucked the flounces of my green school dress neatly around me. I looked back at the office door, which was closed. The door was tall and imposing, just like Miss Mullins. The ceilings were high, floating far above me. The walls echoed their whiteness onto the columns that stood stately, as if holding the secrets of yesteryear and the airy allure of tomorrow.

Two girls, much older than me, made their way up the stairs. They were also in green, not bottle-green like me, more of a sun-lit green, fresh, like a breeze chasing the flowers from a jacaranda tree. Both were clutching satchels, hemlines well below the knees and belts pulled tight into their waists. I pretended not to see them and instead turned to the portraits framed on the walls. All the girls pictured were wearing the same uniforms I'd just seen. There were lots of them, black and white, caught in the crystals of time and stored in the present.

I watched the two girls as they headed away from me. They laughed. They walked quickly. They knew not to run. They left no prints on floors that were polished to a shine and, as I sat there, I noticed there was not a scuff mark anywhere. I'd never seen a school like this before and I knew I wanted to be a part of it.

My mother's eyes were red and puffy when she finally made her way out of the office. We never spoke of that conversation.

It was three weeks later that we received the letter. My mother arrived home brandishing the envelope, with its open, serrated edge, and presented it to me as though the contents were a surprise to all. I had been accepted.

My father was enormously proud. He grabbed me to him and he hugged me close.

"I knew she'd get in."

And so it is that he's driving me back to school after a weekend out. I keep my gaze out the window and as I stare into the darkening middle distance my thoughts are stormy. I hadn't wanted to drive with him. I had begged my mother to take me, but as she explained, she needed to stay home with my brother and sister. And now a dog lay dying, discarded along the side of the R514 like a dirty, disused dish rag.

It was never my choice to be in the car with my father when he'd been drinking. But somehow I so often was. Perhaps he enjoyed the company or maybe he thought that by making it a father-daughter outing we could pretend, and then it would be as if I only imagined the blot in his eyes.

I knew that look well.

"Are you coming with me or not, my girl?" my father would announce without any preamble.

"Where you going?"

"Are you coming with me or not!"

If my mother were nearby I would implore her with my eyes. She'd busy herself.

We both knew. My compliance safeguarded us all.

It was a short journey to the golf club along the tar road. A few turns and we were there.

Once there he'd assure me that we wouldn't be too long.

"I'm just going to have one, my girl," he'd say. "Just one."

But it was never just one.

With a flourish, my father would present me with my first Coke. The waiters, who all knew my name, would bring me the second Coke. And even the third. Sometimes I would be given a packet of Simba chips – smoked beef – or some peanuts.

Then, as time strained the day, I would sit by myself, alone, trying to ignore the discomfort of the hard, unyielding concrete step numbing my bottom. At each creak of the dark wooden door, I'd look up, confident that it would be him at last. When it wasn't, I'd leap to my feet and peer into the gloomy darkness of the bar, trying hard not to gulp in the sluggish air, hanging heavy with sweat and stale cigarette smoke. I'd lean in, tall on my toes, and wave my arms wildly, hoping he'd notice my blonde head as it bobbed about, to remind him it was time to go home.

Sometimes he would notice, and remember. Other times not.

But my eyes were always there to meet his liquid look when he eventually staggered out, unsteady on his feet. Then buoyed with beer, he'd clumsily crush me to his side, circling his arm around me as though we were craftily colluding as one.

"Come, my girl, let's go home," he'd announce happily. As if it had only been a brief stop.

Then we'd begin the treacherous journey home.

We never took the fast, tarred road back. Instead, we'd painfully negotiate the dirt road, my father trying to stay upright behind the steering wheel as we drifted from one side to the other, shadowing the winding river canal. I knew we were almost home when we turned right, lurched over the narrow bridge, and passed Multiplant nursery.

He'd wink at me with a knowing, "We've made it."

I would nod reassuringly and pretend to be won over even though I was sick to my stomach.

My mother never asked how it was.

There was no need.

I am relieved to finally get out of the car when he drops me at the hostel. I quickly make my way to the prep room and seat myself for the mandatory Sunday-night prep session.

After a weekend out, we are expected to write an urbane thank-you letter home, highlighting all we'd particularly enjoyed. We sit there, one behind the other, our heads bent, frantically scribbling letters of thankfulness. We are only to be excused once our letters are written, the envelopes sealed and handed in to the teacher on duty. My pen is poised but I am unable to do it. I am unable to enthuse as I sit there tormented by the images of a dying dog. So I fold a piece of blank paper in an envelope, address it to my parents and hand it in. It is a simple plan. I'll retrieve it from the post before breakfast. But the next morning the messenger has beaten me to it and all I see is a bare space where plumped envelopes once stood.

They are all gone, gone like black cats in the dark.

A letter of ungrateful nothingness has been mailed to a letterbox in Brits.

There is nothing I can do so I make my way to the dining hall.

I soon forget the dilemma of my ungratefulness, as my mouth begins to itch with the cloying, sweet, coppery smell of the loathed fried liver and onions. I choose instead to spoon sloppy porridge into a bowl as I nudge myself in between my friends. We are a group from all over, daughters of farmers, businessmen, miners and diplomats.

I have been at boarding school for eight months and even though I find refuge in that beautiful heritage building among that group of gangly girls, I still find myself battling homesickness. Some days the feeling of longing and the sense of displacement are all-consuming, but fortunately it is a common thread between us all. We find ourselves trying to be big and brave and when that doesn't work out we turn to each other for words of comfort.

But the routine of an organised day offers something of a great distraction as we are roused to the surface early each morning by the matron, waddling down the passage, her broad hips undulating in the dim light.

"*Wakker word!*" she shrieks, her cacophony reverberating across the entire boarding house. "*Wakker word, meisies!*" each word emphasised with a footfall, one flat foot after the other, hitting the cold tiled floor. All the while clanging her polished brass bell.

As early-morning wakings go, it is nothing short of sadistic, but the hours go by quickly and soon we're exhausted from a full day and, drained, we'll slip back into bed.

When night falls I feel safe, the only sound disturbing the dark the occasional vehicle as it accelerates down Park Street, past Loftus Versfeld rugby stadium, and into the distance. I am no longer wetting my bed or biting my nails. But sleep never comes easily and once lights-out is called and everyone has settled in, I creep to my window and, with the weak beams from the street light diffused over my shoulders, I fold myself into the sill, hold my book up high and envelop myself in words. As the night hours drain away, I page past the guilt that prickles like an invisible scar when I fret for my brother and my sister.

And what of my mother – who is looking out for her? Who will pass her a pillow if she is made to sleep outside again?

Twelve

"Hurry," I urge.

"I'm coming!" my sister calls, her voice swept away by the wind.

We are both clutching our blue berets to our heads with one hand, holding the hemlines of our green school dresses down with the other as we rush to catch the double-decker bus into town. The next bus will only arrive in thirty minutes and by then it's too late.

Our laughs are strangled by the warm, dry air as we swing ourselves into the bus and gallop up the stairs to get a good spot at the top. There we collapse onto the blue leather seat, breathless and giggling as the bus lurches forward. It is the best place to sit, enthroned as we are on the apex of the world. It's just the two of us, peering down, scanning the landscape as it changes and shifts around us. And, sitting up high, we gloat at our good fortune. It's a Friday afternoon and we have been granted a special privilege. We have permission to leave the school premises. No one else is permitted out. It is our very own personal triumph.

Boarders are only allowed off the school property once every half-term – the promise of a two-hour excursion that keeps us all on our best behaviour for weeks, lest the privilege be taken away. As soon as the permissions book is signed, best friends set off in groups of two, socks slipped suggestively below ankles and skirts hoisted high above knees, to rush through to the Hatfield shopping centre. It really isn't enough time to keep an eye out for any passing schoolboys, to shop, and then wait for a lull in the queue at the only coffee shop. But once seated, our orders are standard, so it isn't long before a freshly baked waffle is placed between us. With our heads close together, we diffidently divide the waffle in two, squarely split the spoonful of ice cream and carefully carve the clump of clotted cream crushed beneath hundreds and thousands, hanging heavy like a cascade of colourful confetti. And if that isn't enough, each of us sips at a double-thick milkshake between those doughy mouthfuls, oozing stickiness as the sugar-crystal topping melts. It's red, green, blue, white and yellow seeping into each other, our very own sodden syrup of decadence. We savour every single moment, knowing it is a long month until the next two-hour outing.

But there we are, my sister and I, out and about, travelling in triumph, conquering the day while all the other girls are caged behind perimeter walls, sweating it out at compulsory sport. The two of us, on a bus flooded with afternoon sunlight that is broken only intermittently by the scrape of a jacaranda branch as it scratches and grabs at the window as we roll by. The sun, a tree, the sun ... light, dark, light, dark ... all the way into Arcadia.

Once off the bus, we march two blocks down before turning left into a side street, then a short distance on it is up a few stairs into a nondescript building for another counselling session. We aren't here for group therapy, though. We're fortunate enough to be having private sessions with an Alateen addiction counsellor, all part of the Al-Anon fellowship providing support for teenagers from alcoholic homes. It is the first professional intervention and support we've ever known. No one had ever spoken to us about our father's alcoholism before. In fact, it is a subject everyone prefers not to talk about. Who would we go to anyway?

I knew not to phone the police. It was more than once that I had crept into the dining room in the darkened dead of night, to lift my fingers to the black telephone on the sideboard, and make a call to the police station in Brits.

"Please come. My dad is hurting my mom," my voice small and soft as I'd whisper into the handset.

It was always the same loud response in a thick Afrikaans accent: "I'm sorry, young lady, but it's a domestic issue. Our hands are tied." Then, "There is nothing we can do. *Sorrie.*"

It didn't matter how much I silently sobbed.

Our neighbours, the Tellings, were just as helpless when they found me frantically banging on their door. They were already asleep when I arrived. I had taken flight in my pyjamas and felt no pain as the rough stones ripped at my bare feet. The brutality of the beatings had increased over the years and I knew my mother needed help. So I ran. I ran as fast as I could in the black of night, guided by the stars above me, to get to their house, one long kilometre away.

"Mr Telling, please, you need to help us. He's going to kill my mother."

"Let's first have a cup of tea," he'd said, pulling the cord on his gown tighter.

I didn't want tea.

There wasn't time.

I needed to get back to my mother and my brother and my sister.

But I sat there, at the pine table, gripping the pottery mug and drinking the sugared, white tea that Mrs Telling had made for me. It was all calm and quiet by the time Mr Telling eventually took me home.

It seemed there was no one to turn to.

I knew that not even my grandmother would intervene.

We had been staying with her for the December holidays when I ran into her kitchen.

She, my Gan, was standing at the stove in her blue, patterned dress, neatly belted at the waist, stirring her famed oxtail stew. My father's grunts and my mother's howls of pain were braising the afternoon air.

"Gan, please ... do something." I was crying, my words desperate and rushed.

"I can't," she said.

"But you're his mother. He's hurting her. You have to do something!"

Her gold watch, the one my father had given her for Christmas a few years before, a laced handkerchief folded tightly beneath its thin strap, caught the light as she turned her deep-set eyes toward me.

"There's nothing I can do," she said, her words clipped and clear. I had never heard her voice so cold.

The steam of the simmering oxtail stung my throat.

We were on our own.

It was only at boarding school that I learnt otherwise.

Miss Mullins, the headmistress, made it quite clear that her tall, imposing door would always be open to me. She might have been a mother to none but she was deeply committed to 'her girls'. She especially took broken girls to her side, and guided them, and nurtured them, and loved them in her own queenly way.

That was how I got to know Ana.

Ana was three years older than me. She had the saddest eyes I'd ever seen; they were watery blue with edges of steel grey. She was one of six, the only daughter, and it seemed there wasn't enough love to go around in her home. Her life had been one of neglect and disinterest and, after being raped, her world had completely disintegrated – and so she ran away. I had never known that a life could be lived in such pain. All she wanted was for someone to care for her. And Miss Mullins did. She cared. She cared so much that she obtained special permission from the school governing body and brought the much older Ana into the junior boarding house.

Ana knew that she mattered to Miss Mullins, but even that wasn't enough. It couldn't be. Her hurt was too deep. She was wild and, some might say, almost savage, viewing the world around her with a deep, unsettling suspicion. Her blonde hair was short and coarsely cropped, as though someone had carelessly taken a pair of scissors to her head and hacked at her locks in clumps. She was always in her navy-blue school jersey, oversized, long and baggy and hanging well below the hemline of her dress. Her sleeves were always pulled down too, her fists clasping the edges of her jersey, hiding the scars on her wrists. Those scars would be added to while at boarding school.

She was considered reckless and stubborn and many of the girls were scared of her. But she became my friend.

It was an unlikely friendship because there wasn't one iota of the rambunctious rebel within me. I was not defiant. I was tamed. My role was always to broker peace, to be the easy, compliant one. Tantrums and self-expression were provocative. Besides, my mother had too many problems of her own; I knew there was little place for mine.

But knowing Ana taught me one thing: that I was not alone. Her story of sadness gave me some perspective of my own life and I found an acceptance and an understanding that I had not known before. I admired her bravery, the conscious decision she had made to survive when she chose to live another life – one on her own and on her own terms. I also admired her courage, which was especially evident when she came home with me for a long weekend. I thought that was particularly plucky. No one ever came home with me. My house was not a place for friends.

She called it her *Safari Farm Weekend* after a visit to the cheetah and wildlife centre close to our home. Perhaps for her it was a meeting of kindred spirits with those wild cats, together, all of them, viewing life through hooded, slit eyes. Ana couldn't leave them to lie around lazily; she liked to push boundaries and clearly wasn't going to let this opportunity pass her by. She was determined to draw those wild cats closer to her, to see whether she could lure them from their languor and rile them into action. I watched as she grabbed at the mesh fence and rattled it, taunting and teasing them to come closer. They responded as one. They turned to her, dropped their heads, and with icy intent silently broke through the shrubbery, a pack of predators stealthily stalking toward her.

It was the first time I ever saw Ana lose her nerve. As the largest of the cats lunged forward and landed with all its might, bending the reinforced steel fence into her, Ana catapulted as high as she did far. She was still exhaling the residue of its skanky breath and about to dust the sand off her when she approached the adjoining enclosure. As she leaned forward, choking on her nervous laugh, a cheetah cub stuck its paw out and hooked her takkie with a tiny claw. The ensuing scuffle attracted its lactating mother. I suspect a cheetah cub lost its claw that day as Ana leapt for lasting safety.

She left a void in my life when she matriculated, but her departure coincided with my sister's arrival at the school – that, in itself, a great relief. Only my brother remained at home. It would be another year before he too would be sent off to boarding school. Thoughts of his safety gnawed at me. I knew he was angry, afraid, and resentful after having been on the receiving end of so much of my father's violence and self-hatred. My brother, regrettably, would never know the comfort of a similar bolstering hand of support.

Those Friday afternoon sessions with the Alateen counsellor become an enveloping embrace for me and my sister as we share our experiences and gain some insight into the chaos around us. All we had ever known was the determined pull of either my father's drunkenness or his sobriety. We were always teetering on the abyss of one state of his being or another, floundering in the bedlam of uncertainty, unpredictability and the constant unknowing. It was like a clock that was constantly ticking, its pendulum unevenly weighted as it oscillated; a perilous delay between each tick and tock. We lived in flux, anticipating its inevitable unhinging. And more and more unhinged it was becoming, too. Eventually his sobriety would slip through the chambers of time and be relegated to his past, but back then we still hoped for positive change and the addiction counsellor's words offered critical counsel.

She was not what you'd expect of a counsellor. There was nothing cute and cuddly about her. She towered above us, tall and angular, and could quite easily have looked Miss Mullins in the eye. When we shuffled into her office, she needed to only take one or two self-assured strides across the thin carpet to reach and greet us. Her smile was engaging, albeit slightly lopsided as her head was always down, tilted, as though she seldom had need to look straight ahead at others, which meant that her thick fringe kept falling forward and she was constantly flicking it back.

As she sat at her desk, surrounded by colourful, animated self-help posters that had been stuck haphazardly on the walls with Prestik, she encouraged us to speak. She gave us a voice as she listened, heard and asked. She became our soft place to fall. She encouraged us to live in the present and accept that we were helpless to change our circumstances. She took us through the adapted twelve-step programme and offered us the Alateen literature that taught us that our father's compulsive drinking was a disease. A dreadful disease. Debilitating and all-consuming. But it was a disease from which we had to learn to emotionally detach ourselves. She reassured us that we were not the cause of his drinking or his behaviour and that we could not control or change him – only he could do that. She emphasised that the only control we had was over our personal choices in life and that we needed to develop our own potential, despite what was happening at home. She told us that we alone were responsible for our futures and that, ultimately, it would be up to us to write our own stories one day. Her words resonated deeply. But I already knew my story. I was going to be an actress or television presenter, I would write a book one day – and I would never be beaten up.

Thirteen

It was Sunday. The first day after he beat me. Monday would be the second day after he beat me. Not that I consciously counted the days – it would simply become the way I defined myself and my life.

Before and After.

He had taken his hands and divided my life into what was and what would be.

Sunday was the first day – the first day of the After – and there was much to do.

I knew I couldn't languish in my childhood bed all day, overwhelmed by the pain pulsing through me, not just the layers of sharp physical pain, but also the intense hollowness of hurt deep inside me. My sadness and soreness needed to be set aside. I needed to phone my new clients and inform them that I couldn't present their corporate video the next day. I needed to contact the radio station and let them know I wouldn't be in for the foreseeable future. But most importantly I needed to speak to my ex-husband Alex.

"What's wrong?" he asked immediately.

"He beat me," I said, my words distorted and muffled as I tried to say them aloud.

"*Beat you?* How bad?"

"Bad."

It was not easy to talk but I asked that he keep our son with him until the early evening so that I could get back to Johannesburg to salvage my home before he came home.

Alex agreed.

"Don't worry," he said quietly. "We'll do this together."

We'd been apart for three years already. We'd only been dating a few months when I fell pregnant almost seven years earlier and had decided that marriage was the best way forward for our child. We'd uttered marriage vows lightly in the quaint Old Fort Chapel in Durban, knowing that this wasn't going to be a lasting union. We'd got divorced three years later, one lawyer between us. He'd gone to court alone and had consoled me over the phone afterwards, listening calmly, as I sobbed dramatically.

"It's over, Alex. It's a phase of our lives that's over."

All those years later and, as we parented our son together, Alex was still an integral part of my life. I had introduced the two men, but Alex had taken an instant dislike and found him arrogant and condescending, especially after he demeaned Alex at my dinner table one night. I had dismissed it all as incidental rivalry, a clash of egos.

But Alex was aware of at least some of what had happened. He knew I had a restraining order in place. He had seen the damage to my house and my car and we had spoken previously about my safety and the safety of our son. I had assured him that I had everything under control. Clearly, I hadn't.

○

My mother and John drove me back to Johannesburg. It was eerily quiet when we turned into my street. There were no longer any police vans or security vehicles parked along the verge.

John pulled up along the pavement, in front of the white wall with its locked exterior door and its open, gaping centre. The wooden panels hung in splintered shards and greeted us like an open, snarling mouth. I couldn't bring myself to enter through its beckoning emptiness and chose instead to go through my garage and shuffle past the concrete columns that had been rebuilt only a week earlier. They were standing dull and dreary, yet to be repainted.

My footfalls were heavy as I stepped into my entrance hall, dreading what I'd see before me. I hadn't been able to look the night before, but I knew of the destruction.

I didn't know where I would begin with the clean-up operation. I could barely move and, with one eye swollen shut and the other no more than a slit, I couldn't see much either. But as I stepped into my lounge, I could see enough to know that nothing was as it had been left the night before. Nothing.

It was all as it should be … just a little different.

Wilhemina, who worked for me, had taken it upon herself to clean everything up, to restore what had been, to purge the place of any evidence of the carnage. All the damaged furniture was upright and in place. All electronic gadgets, functioning or not, were back on their shelves. Broken ornaments had been swept up and discarded. Glassless photo frames were stacked on top of each other and placed carefully to one side. Everything.

She had done it all.

It felt as though her creased, faded palms were holding me high and I couldn't help myself as the tears fell, knowing I didn't have to bend down and pick up the shattered pieces of my own home, my own life.

All I needed to do was rest until my son returned.

He arrived with his father pulling him on, holding his chubby hand tight, steering him toward me. I never asked Alex whether he'd prepared my son in any way or if it was me wearing sunglasses that made him instantly reticent, but he quickly moved in behind his father and turned his head away from me.

I left him be and instead moved away and allowed them to follow me into the lounge. It was dark, but warm inside. Wilhemina had closed the room for the day, but the heat of the afternoon lingered and a hint of roasted floor polish flushed the air. We sat down, the two of them close together on an armchair and me opposite, on the couch.

"Remember Mommy told you he had problems?" I said to my son softly. "Well, he has," I said before telling him at least some of what had happened.

His eyes opened wide as he watched my lips, listened attentively to the words that flowed from my mouth slowly and simply. His lower lip was caught tight in his little mouth as he blinked back the tears. It had been only one month before that he'd blown out six candles on the blue-and-white racing car cake I had baked and decorated for his birthday party. This was not what I wanted to be telling him now.

"Mommy, can I see your eye?" he eventually asked.

"Yes, you can," I nodded. "I'm going to take my glasses off now," I said slowly, trying to prepare him.

As I lifted them from my face his little hand flailed for his father. He dropped his head deep into Alex's chest, but his words were clear. "Please put your glasses back on, Mommy," he said. "You look so ugly."

I quickly put them back on, my haste belying the hanging heaviness in my heart.

Alex cradled him gently and then looked at me and asked, "What are you going to do?"

"I've laid charges. I'll go to court."

We were both quiet.

I looked away. I saw my two ornamental, wooden ducks. I had bought them years before as a reminder of the wild geese that used to fly over our house when I was a child and how my father complained constantly of the mess they made in the pool. Wilhemina had placed them carefully alongside each other on top of the uprighted TV cabinet. They had lost their place on the glass coffee table and both simply sat there, chipped, forlorn and beakless.

They were a portent to what lay ahead as I became increasingly voiceless and my story was taken from me, but as I sat there bruised and swollen before my son, I didn't know any of this. I trusted the justice system to be fair and reasonable, and believed that laying charges and going to court was the only way.

"If it gets too much, you can come with me," Alex ventured.

He was referring to his imminent departure. He was about to take a five-year political posting overseas and he was kindly offering for me to go with him.

"Thank you. I appreciate it, but you know I can't," I said, trying to smile. I was grateful for his generosity.

"Anyway, it'll be okay," I assured him.

"Well, if you need me to testify I'll come," he said.

"No, you won't need to. I'll be fine," I said, believing my own words. "But thank you."

It was then that my son found his voice.

"How did he hit you, Mom? Like this?" and he threw his small fist into the air.

"Yes."

"Or like this, Mom?" he said, leaning forward, flailing his arms in an upper cut.

"Yes."

"But which one?" he asked. "Which one did he do first?" He didn't wait for an answer. "This one or this one?" he asked again, swinging his hands. "And what happened to the table?" He eyed the glassless coffee table. "Did he hit you before he broke the table?" Then back to me: "Are you sore, Mommy?"

There were so many questions and I didn't want to silence him. I knew that his little mind was working furiously, trying to make sense of it all. His world had suddenly become a scary place, unpredictable and unsafe. And it was going to get even scarier with his father leaving the country in three months' time and him starting primary school. I would need to get him into therapy as soon as possible. As he sat opposite me, silhouetted as one with his father on the armchair, I knew I was his only certainty.

"Come give Mommy a hug," I said, opening my arms. "I'm going to be okay."

I wanted him to know that, despite the bruised eye, the swollen cheek, the aching heart, I was still his strong, dependable mother, that I was still his refuge. His young, vulnerable life might have been forever changed, but as I pulled his small, blond head closer

I silently vowed to do whatever was needed for it not to be forever damaged.

And I held him tight.

Fourteen

"Where you going, Mommy?"

"Nowhere, I'm right here," I said again.

He didn't want to be alone and neither did I. I longed for the sweeping comfort of my aloneness, but I still didn't want to be on my own. I was seeing shadows everywhere. They were morphing over my garden wall, taking shape outside my windows, knocking on my door and fleeing down my passage at night. They were dark, fluid and insidious and I couldn't get away from them. I was seeing them all around me.

He had been arrested as soon as he set foot in the police station but, despite the conditions of the restraining order, had been released on bail almost immediately. I knew he was close – I suspected he was staying a few blocks away – and I was afraid of what he'd do next. He'd warned me to fear for my life. And I did.

I also feared for my son's life, and I didn't want him back at preschool just yet. The teachers knew of the latest developments, just as they'd known for a while that only I, or his father, could collect him at the end of the day. But now, after all that had happened, I wanted to keep him close to my side and always in sight. I tried not to hold on too tight, but sometimes I felt like I was drowning from the fear and as the blackness seeped to the edge of my vision and I gulped desperately at the air, I sealed us in.

I shut the windows and closed the curtains. I locked the doors. I had burglar bars installed and caged us in behind rods of steel. I had my house number painted boldly on my exterior wall for greater visibility so that, if needed, the security company could find me quickly and easily. In the months ahead I would eventually feel it necessary to sell my car, move house and nestle a borrowed firearm beneath my pillow, but for now Wilhemina moved indoors and my son moved into my bed. He was too afraid to sleep in his room, alone, and I was too afraid to let him.

I knew I needed to escape the fear, reclaim some sense of safety. I knew I needed to silence the noise because when the darkness gave way to the light and then slipped back into the black, there was no respite from the visions. It was all I could think of and I was aching from the terror and the tiredness. I needed to put my head down on a pillow far from my life and close my eyes to the recurring images. I needed to let the bruises heal, allow the pain to dissipate. I needed to sleep. I needed to eat. And I needed to get away. So when John mentioned he was going to Kenton in the Eastern Cape for a week I decided that my son and I would accompany him.

John loved to drive. It was as though the stresses of the day tumbled from his shoulders when he turned the key in the ignition. He was a man entranced by the steady, slow vibration of the accelerator beneath his foot and was not averse to taking a scenic alternative in his attempt to extend his driving pleasure. We'd been on holiday in Kei Mouth a few years earlier. It had been a great family holiday of boating, river cruises, water sports, fishing and illicit braaiing on the beach. John was driving us back to where we were staying when what I can only imagine was a flash of inspiration struck him wildly and spontaneously, for suddenly instead of turning left, he turned right, taking us all on a long journey into the unknown. After many hours of winding roads and mountain passes and wanting to throw up from motion sickness I made an oily comment from the back seat about seeing the Mozambican border up front. John was not amused and promptly swung the car onto the first turning we finally came to, one that was signposted East London. He said not a word to anyone all the way home. So I learnt to ask John where he was going before I climbed in behind him. But mostly all roads led to contentedness for John and I was not surprised when he announced he'd collect us at the end of his work day and we'd journey across the country through the quiet of night. John wanted the road to himself. And I was glad of it too.

It was just the three of us in the car, but still I kept my face hidden. My son had not seen me uncovered since he'd asked me to put my sunglasses back on a few days earlier. The large bump on my forehead was still swollen and ugly and the blood that had seeped into the tissues deep under my skin had left my face a livid purple-black. I preferred not to see myself either. I lay hidden in a duvet on the back seat, behind my black lenses, and left it to John and my son, who was sitting tall upfront, to fill the interior with their chatter as I closed my eyes behind the layered darkness and searched for silence.

○

As small towns tend to be, Kenton was quiet, gentle, soothing, and our week soon settled into a healing rhythm. It was only time that would rub the bruises away and ease the pain. Wading through the rock pools and ambling slowly along the beach, the distant waves spraying their soothing saltiness were restorative and the days passed by smoothly. As October drifted into November, it was chilly but despite the cold the clear green waters of the Kariega River drew my son enticingly. It was good to watch him mindlessly swim the current and cross backwards and forwards over the lagoon as he frolicked, diving in and out of the ripples. The hours passed safely on the beach sheltered by the dense Euphorbias with their gnarled leaves oozing a milky, caustic sap.

We spoke a lot, my son and I. I tried to answer his questions simply and clearly.

"Mommy, where is he?"

"He's in jail," I said, hoping for a gust of wind to sweep my lying words away.

Over the days, his fear slowly subsided and finally he asked to see my eye. He looked. He touched. He talked. And I held him close.

"Can I put the cream on your eye, Mommy?" he asked.

I let him lean in and apply the ointment, bravely playing doctor in his attempt to take charge of his own ruptured world. I allowed him his adopted role, knowing it would only be for so long. I would put a time frame to him being my carer. Living beyond his years was not a burden I would allow him to carry. My pain was my responsibility.

Dabbing at my swollen cheek, gently patting at my bruised eye, his small hands on his mother's battered face took me back to another time, to another place. I remembered my mother's pain, I remembered the responsibility I took on my shoulders during those brief futile conversations.

"Please, Mom, please leave him," I plead.

"I can't ... You don't understand ... I love him."

All those times out on the veranda with me listening as she speaks, watching her as she inhales lightly on her forbidden cigarette. Cigarettes that she hides at the back of my dressing-table drawer for me to retrieve when asked. We sit as co-conspirators, on the white wire-mesh chairs, looking out over the veld, as she divests herself of some of her hurt, her words weighty, her breathing shallow. When we hear my father weaving up the road, she scurries back inside to brush her teeth and to remove the evidence of her offense. I rush back inside too, the wire mesh from the chair imprinted down the backs of my legs like a latticed grid, red and itchy to the touch.

And now all these years later, making our way down the beach, occasionally settling down on the sun-baked rocks, all the time soothing my son's fears while allowing my own body to heal, I was determined not to relieve myself of the responsibility of my life and the choices I had made. My son would not be my crutch. He would not be my confidant. He would not be the keeper of deep, dark secrets.

But, as it turned out, there weren't going to be many of those. Deep, dark secrets. It was all soon to enter the public domain.

We were driving back from Kenton when I got the call. We'd passed through the Karoo, through Colesberg, and were on the long, straight stretch heading toward Bloemfontein when I answered my phone.

"Hullo, it's André here. From the *Sunday Times*."

A journalist! Oh my god.

Why would a journalist be calling me?

"Yes," I said tentatively.

"We're doing a story for tomorrow's paper and I'd like your comment."

A story ... tomorrow's paper.

"Yes?" I stuttered, the word coming out strangled.

"It seems there was a fight. Your boyfriend says you lunged at him with a knife. That you stabbed him in the foot."

"He *what?*" I breathed, trying to make sense of his words. "He says I lunged at him? With a knife?"

"Yes, a knife."

"But that's not true!" I cried.

"Well, that's what he said. So that's what we're printing." His words were final.

⊙

This time I couldn't be by myself. I needed someone with me. I phoned my friend Robyn as soon as I got home. She came and sat with me through Saturday night. She waited with me until the early hours of Sunday, until the sun cast its pre-dawn web, bringing no warmth to the new day, and then she drove me to the closest garage a few blocks away. A 24-hour petrol station that would receive the morning papers long before the neighbourhood stretched awake. I was sitting low in the passenger seat when she made her way through the breaking light into the store to purchase an early edition. My red eyes followed her as she picked up the paper, paid and strode back out, the newspaper tucked firmly under her arm. But when she passed it to me, I couldn't take it.

Instead it stayed on her lap and only once we were back in the sanctity of my lounge did she unfold it from its thickness and rouse the damning words from the page.

'Knives come out for TV Star.'

Those were the headlines. Big and bold.

"A love battle between television personality Tracy Going and her boyfriend is heading to the courts," she read out loud. "The thirty-year-old from Brits claims [her boyfriend] beat her, then trashed her home in Parkhurst, Johannesburg. But he claims she stabbed him in the right foot with a knife, causing lacerations to his leg ..."

Robyn's words fractured and faded into one as she read aloud. I had stabbed him in the right foot, causing lacerations to his leg? How? How was that even possible? How could I have stabbed him in his foot? He had been wearing his brown suede shoes. Lacerations to his legs could easily be explained because he'd been wearing shorts when he clambered through the shattered door after my neighbour and his son had kicked it in. He must have scratched himself on the way out. But stabbing? In the foot? And where was the knife?

Her words filtered back in: "... had stitches in his foot."

Stitches!

How did he get stitches? When did he get stitches?

I sat there. Raw. It felt as though each word was tearing at me, ripping open my wounds, leaving me to look down at pink flesh blackened with ink. Dark thoughts swirled around in my head as I considered all that had happened and what might lie ahead. But if those printed words tore at my being, they also reinforced my decision to take meaningful action. It was not so much that my resolve had been intensified, but more that I could not walk away.

That was now no longer an option.

The rest of the day was fraught with despair and tears. The hours passed slowly, the night bringing no calm either; my thoughts gnawed at me and my nerves rendered me ragged. I tried to quieten my mind, knowing that I had to be in the studio early the next morning. It would be my first day back at work. But I tossed and turned in my attempt to calm my fears, my shame, my sadness, myself.

I was just drifting off – finally – when the phone shattered my unrest.

Now what?

I glanced over at the numbers flicking red on my bedside table.

00:40

Well past midnight.

I felt my way down the passage, rushing, needing to answer before my son was woken by the noise.

"Hullo?" I whispered, holding the handset tight between my trembling fingers.

"Drop the fucking charges or I'll destroy you publicly," he snarled, his voice rough and hard.

"Leave me alone," I said. That was all. And replaced the receiver.

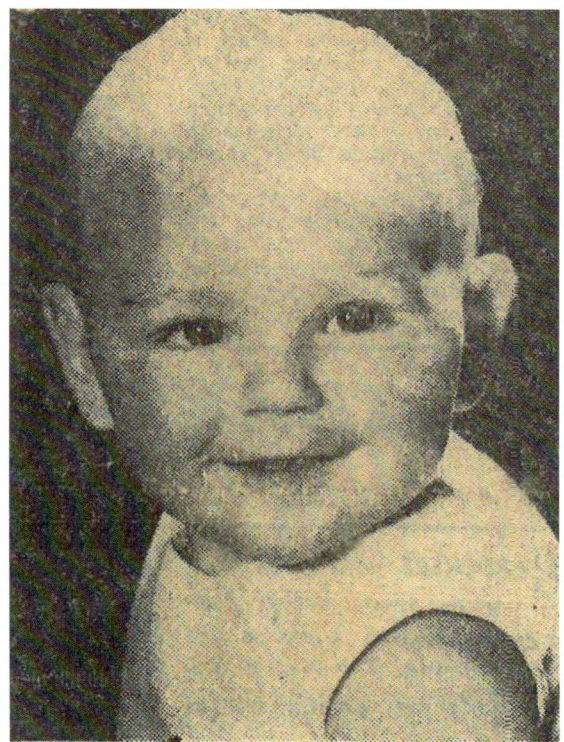

Official announcement of my birth

My father and me *At the lagoon in Kenton, Eastern Cape*

My first day of school outside the first house my father built

The twins, a family friend and me in our bath that doubled up as a swimming pool on sweltering days

The second house my father built

With my grandparents

In the outfit I bought in Durban

The last photograph of my brother David   *Wilhemina and my son*

Bob and me fooling around in the Radio Metro studio

Reading the news on Radio Metro

One of the photographs that featured in the Fair Lady *magazine article*

My son, me and Garp, also from the Fair Lady *magazine article*

The destruction to my garage

The destruction to my lounge

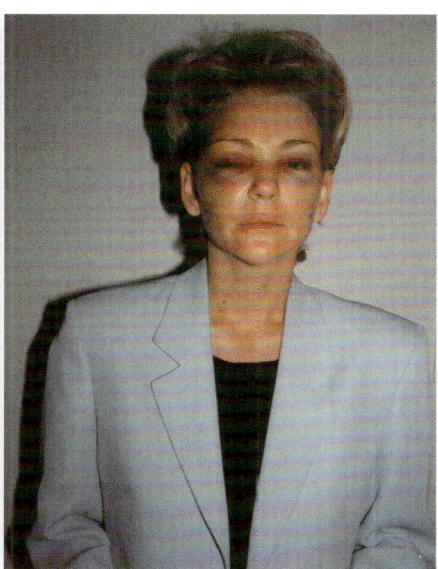

A few days after I was beaten up

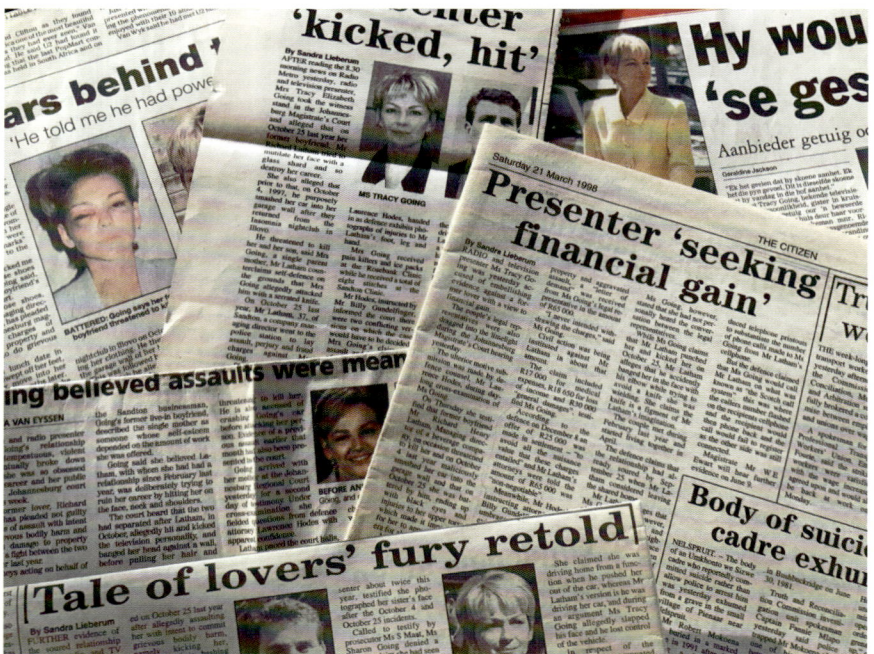

Newspaper clippings

Demonstrators and activists outside the Magistrate's Court

Outside the courthouse speaking to demonstrators and supporters

Me today

Fifteen

I am huddled between my brother and sister, together in the light of ordinariness, when my future comes to me. We are squatting on the coarse, green carpet in the TV room. The square Telefunken is pushed up flat against the stone wall. My mother has drawn the curtains on the day to block out reflections from a sun that is poking its shiny head through the window behind us so the picture that flickers in black and white before us is untainted. The volume is up loud, which means the sound is a little muffled.

We've been sitting there for a while, waiting for the test pattern to disappear and to join in on the countdown as the analogue clock ticks into the hour. Dorianne Berry, one of South Africa's very first TV presenters, finally flickers to life before us. As she smiles her greeting, I turn to my mother and announce, "One day I'm going to be on TV."

It is a realisation that is both simple and absolute.

Over the years I had taken that black-and-white picture and stretched and sculpted and sharpened it into my very own personal, full-colour mental image until it became vivid and vibrant and real. All those years, I visualised myself sitting straightbacked in a studio, groomed, my hair flicked flat and face flawless. I felt the heat as the lights flooded me brightly from above. I saw myself confident and composed, behind a desk, right there in the front line, gazing into the lens, seamlessly cutting between cameras strategically placed across the studio floor trailing their thick, heavy cables. I heard the opening logo as it rolled and crashed through the playback monitors. I imagined it and dreamt it until it ultimately threaded through my being and became a part of me.

And all that positive visualisation, caught in the grander moments of planning my life and setting my goals, had more than paid off.

I had been living my dream, and more.

I had been working behind the scenes on a TV music programme when the presenter, a popular Radio Metro DJ, invited me to read the news on his afternoon drive radio show. He complained that his newsreader had been flirting heavily with the bottle and often didn't make it to the studio on time or even at all. It was the break I hadn't known I was waiting for. Without a word to anyone in the office, I had rushed from the Television building and burrowed my way through the underground tunnel all the way to the Radio block, up past reception and then back deep down, underground to the studio on the far side. I'd made it with minutes to spare. It was the first time I'd ever seen a bulletin. I speed-read through it and then suddenly my name was being announced and I was 'live' on air.

"Good afternoon," I articulated.

"Top stories making the news today …" I said, ending with the same upward inflection of newsreaders I'd heard all my life.

As I read the reams of pages before me I tried to ignore my shaking, querulous voice. I focused instead on the *content* rather than the *delivery*, but I almost lost both my nerve and my words when half way through my reading Koos Radebe, the station manager, barrelled in. I hadn't known who he was, but it was apparent, by his suit, that he was management. I continued reading and pretended I couldn't see him.

He, in turn, had heard an unknown voice on his station and had hurtled down eight floors to investigate.

At the end of my bulletin, Koos stuck out his big, warm hand and said, "Welcome."

The start of my radio career spanning fifteen years.

I had then rushed back the way I had come. Through the tunnel, up through TV reception, past the large sports studios and back into the office, but as I surreptitiously slipped in through the door I heard the sounds of Radio Metro stippling my workplace air.

My boss had, unbelievably, tuned in to listen to the news.

On that day. At that time. To that station.

"You choose," he said.

So I chose.

From there had come the voice work, then the TV work and in between I had freelanced as a crewing agent – when I first fleetingly encountered him. By the time I met up with him to discuss that ill-fated marketing plan, I had been presenting my weekday breakfast show on radio for six years and was also presenting three television programmes.

Lebone – Women on the Move was my primary programme and it kept me busy as I travelled the country meeting and interviewing successful women. It was an inspiring show featuring women who had very often overcome enormous challenges in their determination to succeed. They were all so eloquent and engaging and I was privileged to be sharing in their story.

I was also presenting *One Step Beyond*, an award-winning show about the compelling and fascinating world of technology. Initially, I have to confess, I knew little about IT trends and their breakthrough advancements, but it was innovative and exciting and the best-produced show I would ever work on.

And I was producing and presenting a light-hearted weekly insert on the magazine show *Private & Confidential*. The director, Pieter, who would soon lose his fight against HIV/Aids, had loved random topics and was not afraid to challenge stereotypical thinking. He would select unexplored themes and then provide me with a camera crew. I'd be given carte blanche to interpret it, film it, and edit it in any way I chose. On the surface it was fun and frivolous, but infinitely rewarding to be challenging set thinking.

But my ultimate dream of sitting behind a desk with bright lights beating down on me was coming true with the late-night TV news bulletins on SABC 3.

I had auditioned with the famed Riaan Cruywagen many months earlier. He'd taken me into the news studio, put me on camera and given me a list of seemingly unpronounceable names – all of which I had the advantage of being able to pronounce thanks to my many years of radio newsreading.

As I finished, I turned the sheaf of paper face down and looked at him.

"One day I'm going to be a newsreader on TV."

And I was.

I had been reading the late-night news for a few months already. And to add stardust to the gold at the end of the career rainbow, I was in conversation with the SABC to be signed up as one of the main anchors for the flagship evening news bulletin at 8 pm.

○

But if presenting all those shows had been an affirmation to the power of positive visualisation, I knew that even if I tried to harness the endless power of the subconscious, there was no way to undo the damage to my face. No diligent effort, focused thought or positive introspection could possibly change the way I looked now. It had been two weeks already and my face was still a mess.

"You need your fucking face," he had screamed.

And, yes, he was right. I needed my face.

Monday morning broke early and uneasily. I had been unable to fall asleep after his threatening call. I was terrified of him and even more terrified of what he could still do. I had got up at the crack of dawn to ready myself for work, but I was exhausted. Drained. I was also afraid, mortified, to be appearing in public with my face a swollen mass of livid bruises and scratches.

I had been out and about in Kenton, but only to the beach – just my son and I – and well away from any other public interaction. I wasn't in a presentable state to appear before anyone.

I wasn't even in a respectable state to come before a radio microphone and it would certainly be a while before I could present myself before a camera. But I had already lost half a month's income and I had to work. I was a freelancer, and every day I didn't work meant another day I didn't earn. And the bills were already streaming in. There were doctors' and lawyers' fees, the structural repairs to my home, the household damages and the additional security. It was endless.

So it was that I noiselessly made my way through the Radio reception, hiding my face and my shame. I scurried past security with my hand held high, trying to shade that deep stain that seeped from my eye to my jawline. I was relieved to be the only one in the lift as I made my way up to the newsroom. But what was I going to say when I saw everyone? How would I even begin to explain? When I reached the newsroom, it took only moments to realise there was no need for me to say anything. Everyone knew. Clearly, they had all read the sensational story splashed across the pages of *Sunday Times*.

I quickly took my bulletin and made my way to the studio, past all their warm, sympathetic glances. I knew everyone was trying hard not to stare. I, in turn, smiled and greeted and pretended. But I didn't want to be there. I didn't want to be exposing the bruises on my skin, the shadows in my heart. I didn't want anyone seeing my sadness and my heaviness and my pain.

When I got to the studio I lifted my head and slipped in as though there was nothing unusual about wearing big, black sunglasses underground before the darkness had completely surrendered to the light and before the morning clock had even struck six. I took my place in my chair and, once the news jingle had played, I opened my mouth and read the news slowly and clearly. I enunciated carefully so that the listeners wouldn't know there were swollen storm clouds in my mouth.

And somehow I managed. I was back on radio.

But it was impossible to go on camera. That I couldn't manage.

My co-presenter on *One Step Beyond* stepped in to present all my inserts for the following six weeks. *Private & Confidential* rearranged the show format to exclude me until I could return. But my primary show, *Lebone – Women on the Move*, would need me back, and soon too. So it was that after only four weeks I was left with no option but to appear on camera. They had a few inserts that had been prepackaged and another presenter had stepped in to fill the gap, but they would need me in the studio to record the main links. I was, after all, the face to the show.

Lloyd, the producer, felt we could do it. My bruises could be camouflaged with thick coatings of Kryolan stage makeup. But it was the eye that was the real problem. The black-and-green marbling on my face could be covered, but after four weeks my eye was still a haemorrhaging web of ruptured vessels bleeding its rawness across the sclera. My eye looked like a sad, lonely, dying coal, a fiery red as it burnt its despair. It was also leaking a watery wetness that I was constantly dabbing at with a limp tissue. We all agreed that no viewer would want to look at that.

But what could we do?

Lloyd found a solution.

"We'll film you in profile," he said. "We'll take your hair and coil it over your face, like this," he went on, gently twirling a curl between his fingers.

Lloyd had started his career as a hairdresser.

So I went into the makeup room to have thick foundation lathered on in layers and my eye cleverly covered in colour. My hair was styled and set in swirls across my cheek. Cameras were positioned far back across the studio floor and I was filmed at a great distance, on very wide shots, with my head tilted in profile. We filmed the studio links for a few episodes, which bought some reprieve until the next recording.

I was so grateful to those producers and directors who stood by me, who propped me up until I could rely on my own strength and determination. But the truth of it is that, for the most part, work dried up and my income was slashed dramatically. The reasons, it appeared, were twofold. Firstly, I was simply unable to work, and then there were those who preferred not to work with me at all. It seemed there were many who were afraid to be tainted by the horror and filth of my domestic violence matter and it would be many, many months before any new contracts came in.

I would also never get that call to sign the evening news contract.

It would be a full year before the news editor passed me in the corridor and had the courtesy to mumble, "Sorry I didn't return your calls," he said, not looking me in the eyes. "But we couldn't touch you."

Sixteen

Everywhere I looked I saw scrubbed faces crowded together as they lined the walls, jostling for position in an uncoordinated dance of rubbing shoulders and moving legs. Cheap, unpolished shoes scuffed nervously at the dark floors. We were acknowledged with slight smiles and imperceptible nods, but still no one moved to open a gap, to allow us in. So we stood to one side: my mother, my lawyer, Sheryl and I.

It was the first time my mother and Sheryl had met and they spoke softly over hushed whispers and scraping heels. I tried hard to listen and even harder to distract myself from my gnawing fear. It seemed the yellowed walls were closing in.

The steel doors to the courtyard were open but still a stuffy desperation circulated between the dust and the dying barbs of Lifebuoy soap. Perhaps it was just me who struggled to breathe.

It was Monday, 8 December 1997, but I was impervious to its summery promise. This was my first court appearance. And the first time I'd see him since he'd pummelled my life apart. It wasn't the first time I heard from him, however. I'd heard his voice when he'd called, long after midnight, his message clear:

"Drop the fucking charges or I'll destroy you publicly."

By then he'd already left me no choice.

And now we were here.

My mother had left Brits in the dark. Although it was unnecessary, it was impossible to dissuade her and she would continue to arrive an hour or two early. She insisted that she was reluctant to negotiate rush-hour traffic on her own, but I knew that she didn't want me to arrive at the court alone.

It was to become our court morning ritual.

Before leaving for court I had read the 08:30 bulletin in a rush, my words strangled and inconsequential as I thought of the day ahead and my mother waiting outside in the parking lot. The morning air was clear and warm by the time I stepped out of the Radio Park building to meet her and soon we eased our way through the busy streets of the city centre and the morning traffic, to the court dominating the city's lower end.

We had arrived at the Johannesburg magistrate's court to find my lawyer, Sheryl, standing in the shadow beneath the columns. Her black gown hung sober over her arm, her smile ready. She had no official capacity in the criminal trial. Her brief was simply to collect as much relevant information as possible for the civil case to follow, when her role would be more defined.

But she was to become far more than just a detached legal observer. She was my constant companion and there were many times I clung to her as though afraid of getting lost. Even in the middle of the night, she was never more than a phone call away.

That first morning, I was grateful to be following her into the maze of the court.

Our footsteps echoed as we made our way through dimmed, convoluted passageways in search of the prosecutor. We eventually tracked him down to his office, where he was locking his door, and after hurried introductions and a quick summary of the procedures scheduled for the morning, he directed us to the allocated court and rushed off, clutching armfuls of other people's case files. He was Prosecutor No. 2.

Prosecutor No. 1 had already passed through my life.

When we met at the very first briefing, I had immediately taken to her, drawn to her narrowed features, expressionless face and thin, pursed lips. I could envisage her puckering them tightly as she sucked the accused's words in, then swirling them around like vinegar before spitting them back out. But it hadn't only been her bony shoulders, her terse manner and the sharp shape of her mouth that I had found so reassuring. It was also her unhesitating confidence in the merits of my case. The bruises on my face told my story.

Then she had phoned and announced that she was pregnant.

She was withdrawing from the case entirely. Her maternity leave would coincide with the trial, which meant that the case could be compromised. She said it was the only option, that there really was no other way, but I'd be more than satisfied with Prosecutor No. 2.

The change was unsettling. I had sat before her in her office, my face battered, my eye still swollen and mottled, and I had told her everything. I'd shared all the shameful details and, in the process, given her much of the little I had left. Now I wanted her as my prosecutor. I wanted her fighting in my corner, even if I thought motherhood would soften her edges. Besides, surely nine months was too long. Wouldn't we be done before then?

But that was not for me to decide.

It hadn't bothered me that her first language was not English – somehow, the precision of words hadn't seemed essential for clear interrogations. This, however, was not a confidence that I transferred to Prosecutor No. 2. Although he seemed pleasant enough, I feared he'd be mangled as he stumbled and searched for argument and meaning. And it was on his brisk instruction that we stood outside the courtroom waiting for our matter to be called.

We hadn't been there long when the moment I'd been dreading for weeks finally arrived. The man who'd chosen to hurt me was advancing down the corridor, his attorney at his side. Huddled together, their faces drawn tight in whispered deliberations.

I'd thought endlessly about how I wanted to respond to this initial encounter. I wanted to stand tall, to appear composed and unafraid. I didn't want my bruises to be visible. I'd hid the last of them under make-up before I'd left for the studio. It was a shallow covering to what lay inside, where deep down I was black and blue. But I didn't want him to know how broken I really was. I wanted him to think I was brave, not thwarted.

So I kept myself steady as I watched him approach.

But, as I drew him to me with my eyes, I knew I was also desperately searching for some sign of remorse. I wanted so badly to know that he was sorry for what he'd done. I only needed a peek, a glance, a quick acknowledging look. There was nothing.

He strode past me, his attorney alongside him, as though he had no need for explanation or apology.

I stepped back, unable to hold my stance, shrivelling inside. From under lowered lashes, I followed his steps, along the gleaming floor, parallel to the painted black trim leading out into the courtyard. I saw how, once outside, he fumbled in his pocket, then bent his head and lit his cigarette, before tossing his shoulders back, lifting his chin and inhaling deeply.

My mother took my arm. Her words touched the emptiness in me.

"How you feeling?"

"I'm okay."

My answer sounded hollow, even to me.

We stood, quiet.

"State versus Ngwenya," an unfamiliar voice broke our silence.

It was the court orderly calling out another name into the corridor.

We were surrounded by constant movement as an endless stream of people silently shuffled in and out of the courtrooms. Occasionally, lawyers would pass by: ethereal beings moving in the opposite direction, heads down and purposeful, their black gowns swishing importantly and rubbing gently at what lay beneath.

Still we watched and waited.

Suddenly all the doors along the passage opened, as though a siren had screeched a silent alert. The noise was thunderous as people squeezed themselves out, shoving and pushing in their rush to be free. We stepped back to avoid the milling stampede.

"What's happening?" I asked Sheryl, my voice a little high.

"It's 10:45."

"Yes?"

"It's tea time," she trilled.

Tea time. Another uninvited ritual.

Tea time soon ended. Raised voices dropped quickly and the passage around us emptied as courtrooms sucked the now-subdued back in. Then Prosecutor No. 2 hailed us to the door. Signalling us inside, he instructed us to take a seat on the benches and to wait for our matter to be called. There was only one other case ahead, he assured us. It really wouldn't take long.

The court was smaller than I'd imagined it would be. Untidy. Mismatched chairs all over the place as though they'd been thoughtlessly discarded. Dark, wooden tables stood to one side. They were skew.

It was even darker than it had been out in the corridor. And noisier too. The condensed coughs, shuffling shoes and rustling papers seem to press together loudly. To me it lacked any sense of order: it was hard to think justice would prevail in the chaos.

The magistrate entered and took his place behind the high teak-wood railing, his gown sagging heavily forward, pulling his shoulders round, as he peered down from his raised bench into his shadowy domain.

Nothing was as I had expected.

I had never been in a courtroom before. There hadn't been a need. Although I had spent a morning outside one many years previously.

◯

After twenty years of marriage my mother has finally found the courage. My parents are getting divorced and I have agreed to testify. I am in court as a witness, to take an oath swearing to my father's shortcomings. All that is required is that I hold my hand up and solemnly swear to tell the truth, the simple, short truth. But perhaps the truth is never simple.

I am eighteen years old and I am more than willing to do it.

I am with my mother at the High Court in Pretoria. It has taken much to finally get there.

I am the one who phones to have my father removed from our

home. It has been a while since he has been able to care for himself. He has become so unhinged over the years that he is now a threat, not only to himself and to us, but to others too. I call the police but they aren't able to help. Then I phone the hospital. They agree to send an ambulance to collect him and clean him up. But when the ambulance personnel arrive, my father refuses to go.

"What's going on, my girl?" he asks, the panic clouding his eyes.

"You have to go, Dad."

"What's happening?" he says, confused and uncertain.

"They're taking you away."

He doesn't ask why.

"I'll only go if you take me, my girl."

I nod and turn from him. I know his game, but still ... I don't want to see the tears on his sunken cheeks.

There are no flashing red lights as I slip in behind the ambulance and follow it to Brits. We are at the admissions desk before my father announces that he will not allow himself to be admitted without an overnight bag. He insists that he needs toiletries and clean clothes. What for? Why the need for dignity now? I bristle. But after some negotiation and a promise that he will return, I drive him all the way back to collect his few belongings.

After his brief stay in hospital, it is agreed that he needs further psychiatric observation. His mental and physical collapse, and ultimately his complete disintegration, follow.

I go to court to share the story of my father's shame.

It isn't that he didn't want things to be different. He has, over the years, in his own indomitable way, tried to pull himself together. There have been failed stints at rehabilitation at Castle Carey, in Akasia, a suburb in the north of Pretoria. And each time he packs his suitcase to go, we believe that this time it will be different, this time he'll make it. But he doesn't. He can't. We aren't enough. And, eventually, it is easier for all of us to simply let go.

That's when we stop seeing him.

He gets lost in and around and past us. He lives among us like a drunken ghost.

He stops caring too. About us. About himself. About anything. And in between he even loses the urge for his angry, violent binges. It requires too much. And from there he slowly disappears into his drunkenness until he is in a permanent state of steady insobriety. If he staggers, and falls, he remains where he is. He picks himself up only when he wants to. Or when he is finally able. The blood dries unevenly on his face, until it is cracked and flaked, and remains unnoticed. It works better that way, because then we can pretend we don't notice either. We don't have to worry that he is unwashed and dirty or that his hair has grown long and hangs in neglected strands. It means we didn't have to care either. Or be ashamed.

In the end, there are few words between us. It seems a lifetime ago since he last found me in his glassy eyes.

"Yesh, my girl," he slurs, his words coming out before he can find me, his look always delayed. Coming after. Too late. Trying to focus. "You shink I'm a rubbish."

"Yes, you are, Dad. You are a rubbish."

I spit my words, unkind and uncaring; knowing that my father is still conscious enough to flinch.

But I know that when he steps into the High Court in Pretoria he will have cleaned himself up. He would have needed *one* or *a few* to calm his nerves, but he would have washed, combed his thinned hair into place, using his hand to flatten a few hairs over the dome of his head. He would have shaved the peppery-grey stubble from his drawn cheeks. He would have worn his beige, polyester trousers – the pair with the cigarette burn, because they don't crease – and he would have tucked his faded, short-sleeved, checked cotton shirt tightly into the back of his trousers, but it would have still crept out. He would have pushed it down with his thin arms before entering the court, leaning forward into his unsteady gait, holding his briefcase tight.

My mother had given the briefcase to him as a gift many years earlier, and he is seldom without it, especially towards the end. He carries it about as if its hollowness is packed full of papers of great importance, as though the shiny, tanned leather bag is tangible proof of a prosperous life, one that has been well lived. We, his children, mock him behind his back for his empty briefcase. Our father: slumped in his chair in the lounge, the curtains half-drawn, the tired afternoon sun casting its weak rays over him like a spotlight on a vacant stage, his hollow briefcase beside him.

But today in court that briefcase won't be empty. It will be filled with significant legal documents. I have been told to wait in a small room opposite the courtroom. The details have faded in my memory, but I remember that when proceedings finally get underway, I drift over to lean casually against the frame of the courtroom door, pretending that I am not trying hard to decipher the muffled words on the other side. I hear nothing that makes any sense.

Twenty years. Why? Why has it taken so long for my mother to find the courage?

In the end, that judge decides he is able to grant the divorce without putting me through the ordeal of testifying.

◯

The magistrate I was facing now would not spare me, I knew that much. I knew, too, that my ordeal would not be today. Today was procedural. Today we'd agree to go to trial and the court date would be set for after Christmas. We would let the holidays come and go. We would start in March. Five months after the event.

I heard the next matter being called.

"State versus Dlamini."

I looked up to see a slight young man being called to the front.

I recognised him.

I'd seen him outside. Between the weak smiles and the mumbled pleasantries, our greeting had hung delicate and brief.

Now he was standing opposite the magistrate.

I listened carefully.

A hijacker?

A hijacker!

I had smiled at a hijacker. I'd been giving a hijacker knowing, sympathetic glances all morning. And not only him! Each time anyone stood up outside in the passage, I silently wished them all the very best as they entered the courtroom. How many out there actually deserved their freedom? Were they all criminals? Not just petty thieves. Hijackers. What else? Murderers? Rapists? All sitting, slouching and standing about. And we'd been milling between them all morning.

Victims and violators.

As though we weren't already all wretchedly forged into one.

Seventeen

I walked out into the sweltering afternoon, knowing that this was only the beginning. The midday sun hung heavy. The shadows beneath the steps had blistered and gone. I felt the burn on my face. It was hot and dry, but as I stepped out into the heat, I calmed myself with the thought that everything was finally in motion and that in three months' time I would be testifying and telling my story. Then he would take the stand to defend himself and it would quickly be over.

I had been so afraid to see him, afraid of being put back into harm's way. I knew that I should be safe in the courtroom but, even so, I wasn't entirely convinced. He'd scoffed at the restraining order, he'd broken his bail conditions and had warned me repeatedly that he wouldn't leave me alone.

"I've put a hit on you ..." he'd said. "You have a child ... Six months, one year ... I've got time." He continued: "I have money. I have power. You have nothing."

And, so far, he'd given me no reason to doubt him.

Even though I hadn't been alone with him in that bleak courtroom, it had been unnerving to be so near. I was intimidated by his presence, his long strides, his loud voice and his rough laugh. But most of all, I was frightened of what he could still do.

We had hung back after the court session: my mother, Sheryl

and I. I wanted to speak with the prosecutor to get a clearer understanding of what lay ahead. But I also wanted to delay my exit. I wanted to avoid bumping into him in the parking lot outside. I'd seen enough of him already and had been left shaken and as afraid as I had ever been.

I left for home utterly exhausted.

I fetched my son from school and we spent the afternoon indoors.

My life had become significantly smaller, more secluded, over the previous few months, shrinking to just beyond my house and its high exterior wall. I lived inside, the doors and windows tightly shut. Apart from the court appearance, the early-morning trips to the radio station and the occasional TV shoot, my life had narrowed to a terrifying two-kilometre radius.

When I drove my son to his school or to his therapist, I looked ahead and behind, my eyes constantly darting to the rearview mirror, down side streets. When I needed to go to the supermarket just a few streets away, I crept along the aisles. Otherwise Wilhemina went over the road to the Texas café for the basics. I kept myself hidden, between destinations dictated by necessity. I went nowhere unless it was imperative and I always made sure that I was home before dark descended.

I knew that my fear of him was changing who I was.

So my son and I spent the evening locked indoors and because the morning in court had worn me thin, we went to bed early. My eyes had long since drooped from exhaustion when, just before midnight, my phone woke me.

Please don't let it be him.

Half asleep, I stumbled down the passage.

"Hullo," I said, my words coming out in a choked whisper.

"I'm a reporter from *The Star*."

Another reporter.

"Yes?" I managed.

"Do you have any comment about the charges that have been laid against you?"

Charges? He'd laid charges against me.

"No," I said dropping down into the chair, trying to understand his words, heavy with an Afrikaans accent.

"No, I have no comment ... What's your name again?"
"Jack Hide."
Jack Hide from The Star.
A reporter? So late.
Jack Hide ...
The name had a ring to it though.
Dr Jekyll, Mr Hyde.

Dr Jekyll, the fictional character who takes a potion to become the animalistic Mr Hyde? Was this another tale of a man with an alternate personality? Was it him conspiring to terrify me or was there really a Jack Hide writing for *The Star*?

Charges laid against me.

It was too much to take in.

As his words settled over me, I stayed where I was. I knew I couldn't sleep. I sat there all night until the darkness finally lifted. Only then did I get up and go to work.

As soon as my radio show was over and I was alone, I called *The Star*.

"Do you have a reporter by the name of Jack Hide?"
They didn't.

⊙

"I have the details," said Investigating Officer No. 1.

When I had received his threatening call at 00:40 a few weeks earlier, I had contacted Investigating Officer No. 1 to report it. I had no physical evidence of the call so he suggested that a call-tracer be activated on my phone line. That meant that all incoming numbers could be identified if necessary.

"I've traced the call," he announced. "It's an unlisted number."
"Yes," I breathed.
"I've traced it to the Norwood Police Barracks ..."
The police!
"... to a Detective Potgieter."
Potgieter? The name sounded familiar.

Pottie.

I remembered how he'd gone to meet Pottie to borrow a trailer for a delivery. I hadn't thought anything of it when he laughed and said that if he was ever in trouble, he always had Pottie. Clearly, it seemed, Pottie had met his expectations.

I didn't know Pottie. I had no idea what he looked like and no understanding of what he was capable of doing, but I couldn't leave it be. My silence would be a weapon for him and the accused.

I phoned the Norwood police station. Not there.

I phoned the Hillbrow police station.

I made an appointment to see the station commander. His office, 10:00. I parked in the street, one littered with plastic, shards of broken glass and cigarette butts. I crossed over the road, away from the urban slums and their underworld of crime, and made my way into the police station. I sat opposite the station commander at his desk and I told him of the intimidation, the restraining order, the court case, the bail conditions, the calls, the threats … and now Pottie.

I didn't tell him of my crippling fear, of the interminable sleepless nights, my inability to eat. I didn't want him to know any of this. I wanted him to believe that I would take this matter further if it was not dealt with appropriately.

The station commander phoned me a week later. In his deep voice, he informed me that there had been a disciplinary hearing. Detective Potgieter had initially dismissed my complaint and denied any involvement but, on hearing that the call had been traced to his lodgings, he changed his story. He adapted it, suggesting he was concerned about me and that he had actually phoned to warn me.

"But he didn't phone to warn me. He's lying," I said.

"Well look, that's what he said."

"But it's not true," I insisted.

"Umm, well … I've done what I can," the commander mumbled into the receiver.

At my continued insistence, he finally agreed that it was a questionable explanation. He denied, however, that he was closing ranks, and assured me that Pottie had been sufficiently castigated, and presented as resounding evidence the fact that Pottie had received a small, monetary fine.

But a policeman phoning me late at night, pretending to be a reporter, was not such a cheap matter for me. This was another violation, and I felt even more threatened than I had before.

My home had long stopped being a carefully constructed sanctuary. My sense of safety had been dragged out of me many months earlier when I had been hauled down the passage and into my room with a hand fisted tight around my hair.

I'd learnt long ago that danger comes from within. That it watches us as we bath. It holds the knife when we cook. It dangles the telephone cable as we talk. It strides down the passage when we sleep.

But Pottie was different.

Detective Potgieter was not a threat from the inside. He was on the outside and I didn't know exactly where that was, what that meant. He had taken an oath, sworn to uphold the law, but clearly he thought he was above it, he could threaten and intimidate me. Now I had reported him, I had taken him on, challenged him.

I had to shield myself – from both of them.

And so I put my home on the market. My ex-husband, Alex, moved in and Wilhemina returned to her private quarters outside.

They became my fortress: Wilhemina on the outside. Alex next door, in the room beside me. My son and my dog, Garp, in my bed, close to me at night. The doors between us and the outside locked, secured.

During the day I guarded myself where I could, but mostly I stayed inside.

○

Christmas passed quietly and safely. And by the time Alex left in January for his political posting in Europe I felt stronger, more assured, less anxious.

My friend, Robyn, phoned one day and invited me to join her for tea.

"You need to get out."

She was right.

It had been months since I'd deviated from my schedule and it was about time. I needed to extend my boundaries. So we met at Robyn's favourite spot, Walnut Grove in Sandton City. She loved high tea and the restaurant, located on a bridge over the walkway, served teas with an array of delicate pastries and dense tarts. We sat at one of the small, round tables that dented the plush carpet and were served by a waiter who'd worked there for decades.

It felt good to be out, to allow myself to let my guard down a little, good to be drinking tea and talking to my friend as a piano tinkled in the background. We had known each other since we were twelve years old. We had been together at boarding school. She knew me well and there was no need for me to defend myself, so we chatted, we laughed and I forgot.

It was the right thing to have done. I was glad she had persuaded me to step beyond the comfort zone I had so painstakingly, so methodically, reinforced over the last while, and my step was nimble as I walked away. But the light fell fast as I stepped into the parking lot. Suddenly the afternoon was drained of all colour. I had parked close to the entrance and I saw it as soon as I neared my car.

CUNT

The word had been etched across my windscreen. Scrawled in capital letters. From one side of the glass to the other.

I rushed forward to rub the obscenity away. But as I touched it I felt its powdery, sticky grit. It had been written in glue.

I scratched at it, but my fingers came away dry.

As the panic rose in my throat, it felt as though there were hands clasped around my neck, choking me in an icy grip. They were his hands.

He's done this.

I whirled around, scanned the shadows lurking beneath the columns.

Nothing.

I heard car doors slamming, footsteps. I smelt burning tyres and hot petrol. It all seemed so close.

Where is he?
Is he watching me?
How did he know I was here?

My eyes searched the cars, the empty spaces.

But I couldn't see him.

I crouched low as I fumbled for my keys, slipped the door open and climbed into my car. I locked the doors.

My fingers were numb on the steering wheel. I wiped my hands on my knees and turned the key in the ignition.

Where is the exit?
I have to find the quickest way out, I have to get away, I have to get home!
My child is alone with Wilhemina.

I saw nothing as I sped down William Nicol highway. I focused only on the road ahead as I tried to get some distance between his violence and my self.

It seemed there was no end to his terror.

I'll phone Sheryl, my lawyer, when I get home.
I'll move house.
I'll get rid of my car.
I'll not let him find me.

Eighteen

"There's one," announces my mother excitedly. "There, there! Follow him."

But I've already seen him; his bloodshot eyes squint into the morning sky, his mouth pouts into a sharp whistle, his hand flicks furiously as he directs us into a side street.

"Thank you," I say, shrugging him off, wanting to cut his inevitable words.

"I look nicely," he bows slightly, his hands cupped, determined to have his say.

My smile is vague as I hand over the stipulated amount, not concerned whether he is a self-appointed guard to the open lot or not, just grateful that my car is secure and that I am no longer negotiating the unfamiliar, early morning traffic, vehicles crossing erratically around me, closing me in.

Diagonally opposite us is the now-familiar three-storey building. The magistrate's court in Johannesburg – an enormous, impenetrable massif dominating four city blocks. And despite the sun warming its eastern façade, the brick, carved granite and chiselled stone stand cold and stern. There are rows and rows of identical frosted-glass panes, every single one firmly closed to the day.

It seems so immutable. So solid. So big.

I stay where I am.

"I don't know if I can do this, Mom."

"Yes, you can. Yes, you can …" she tutts, taking my arm and guiding me from the dusty gravel to the pavement. Crisp, dry leaves brush at our feet and crackle underfoot as early autumn whispers, reminding us that nothing lasts.

We cross over Fox Street.

We walk up the stairs saying nothing; we pass two bronze statues, weathered green. They look north, standing sentinel on either side of the lofty wooden doors, impassively keeping guard beneath the columns of the grand entrance.

Only one door is open. My mother steps into the dark first. I follow slowly, cautiously, reluctantly.

It is Thursday, 19 March 1998.

The start of my court case. Today I will finally be telling my story.

As we make our way across the marble landing, down into the criminal courts below, I am confident of the minutiae. The details constantly replay in my head, ricocheting and crashing in all directions as I relive again and again what has happened, mostly with exquisite, exhaustive accuracy. As I follow my mother's quick steps, I am certain of my truth. I have yet to reread the statement I'd made months earlier, but I know that is unnecessary … I can never forget.

Sheryl meets us and once again leads us through the dimness to the prosecutor's office for a final briefing, this time with Prosecutor No. 3.

Her name is Sandra. She is young and feisty. Her blonde hair hangs shiny and straight, unlayered, onto shoulders that are sure, not yet weighed down by her new, black gown. Her back is ramrod straight, as though reinforced by an impassioned belief in the nobility of her work. Her step had been purposeful when she came to meet me a few weeks earlier, right after I was informed, without much explanation, that Prosecutor No. 2 had been moved to another matter.

"Don't worry," she'd said, her glossy lips shining, her smile warm. "It'll all be fine."

After a brief interchange, Sandra scuttles into the courtroom to arrange her documents and order her busy mind. She is joined by Investigating Officer No. 2, to whom I have just been introduced.

We are still lingering outside in the passage when the accused and his defence attorney make their entrance. Neither of them walks quietly – perhaps they simply don't feel the need. As the soles of their shoes strike the floor, their matching lockstep pounds out a forceful rhythm that carves a path through the crowd in the passage. Their arms swing widely, in unison.

I recognise his new attorney immediately. He is a criminal defence attorney. I know him from the society pages in the Sunday newspapers. He has a reputation for being one who prides himself on representing high-profile cases, a man drawn to fame and celebrity like a coiled cobra to a flute.

I had been upset to hear that he had hired a man who ached so to be in the public eye. He had previously warned me to drop the charges "… or I'll destroy you publicly", but somehow I had thought he'd be more discreet and choose a more inconspicuous attorney. It is ridiculous really that, despite everything, I still believe he might have another side, that he might be more restrained. I have clearly miscalculated his desperate need to defeat me at all costs. He has very deliberately selected an attorney who makes no apologies for the fact that he doesn't like to lose.

Behind them is the defence advocate. I do not recognise him.

If circumstances were different I might have admired them as they tramped toward the courtroom, all so swift and sure. The accused and his attorney, head and shoulders above everyone else. But as I stand there with my eyes fixed, I want to flee. I want to get as far away from them as I can, but it is impossible, so I steel myself. I take strength from my surrounds, knowing I am protected among those around me, and I draw myself up a little straighter.

I had carefully selected my outfit the day before: a pale jacket with lightly padded shoulders and slim-fitting trousers. It is one of my newsreader suits, muted, nothing that would compete with the screen or the studio framed behind me. It has been tailored especially for me. I've only worn it once before and the fabric is still hard and unyielding as it hides my thinness, but I hope that as I stand tall in my high heels I at least appear confident.

He is in his navy blazer, white shirt, silk tie, chinos and brown suede shoes. It is the same costume, the same disguise he was wearing when he arrived at the police station soon after he'd beaten me up. It is the same outfit he was wearing when he had first appeared in court five months earlier. I remember when he bought it.

He had bought it for my thirtieth birthday party. It was a reason to celebrate and he was my partner.

I had reserved a dining room at a small, boutique hotel close to my home. I'd been considering the venue for months, long before we'd first met. I'd unashamedly wanted my party to be a glitzy affair. And it had been. The hotel, with its mix of urban chic and contemporary lines, opening out into a dark, green garden, was the ideal setting. An extension of my life at the time, dazzling and uncomplicated. He had bought a single-breasted navy jacket and beige chino pants for the occasion. My eyes had been bright when we walked into the dining room together. Him, dashingly elegant in his new ensemble, and me, sleek in tight, black velvet. My hand had rested lightly on his arm, laying claim.

It seems an eternity has passed since those heady days when anything outside of him was an intrusion, when all that mattered was just being with him, back when his shirt collar was still stiffly crisp, edges unfrayed.

But everything has changed. All of it.

He is gone.

I now cradle a firearm beneath my pillow, the catch on safety.

I no longer drive the same car.

And I have moved to another suburb, to a place he doesn't know.

We have moved to a house three doors away from my son's school. It is an unsightly place, its brick border unpainted and window frames peeling, but it is in an unknown location, behind heavily trellised burglar bars, security doors that snap shut behind us. I feel safer, and within walking distance to his school, my son, more certain.

But I still live as though I am always being followed, followed by him, by the past he has burdened me with. I am haunted by the frightening uncertainty of my future too. When his fists tore into me, my career stalled and it hasn't yet recovered, and I am scraping and scrounging as all the unexpected expenses that followed the attack cripple me. Desperation will force me to start a training company for aspiring television presenters and this will become an essential financial lifeline.

But standing there in that passage, waiting for the court session to begin so I can be called to take an oath, it is inconceivable to think how everything in my life has changed. There is so little that is not different.

But it is mainly me that has altered.

I am no longer the same.

And nor will I ever be.

○

Court reporters and other intent media have filled the back benches by the time my mother, Sheryl and I enter. The front row is where my friends are sitting: Karen, Estie, Robyn and Katherine. Sue, from *Fair Lady* magazine, who has yet to become my friend and one of my most valiant supporters, is also there.

My mother and Sheryl join them on wooden benches, benches that will soon become harder as the court case trudges on.

My place is alongside Sandra, Prosecutor No. 3, and as I sit down I hold myself away from the edges of the chair, trying not to touch the dirty maroon fabric.

The magistrate's footsteps are drowned by whispered greetings and the innocent chatter of those who have come to watch.

"May the court rise," the court orderly calls, disinterested.

It is only after this feeble announcement that quiet eventually settles and everyone stands.

But perhaps it is the magistrate himself who inspires so little notice.

He is flexed forward as he shuffles in through the door, his shoulders dragging him down. I can't see his eyes, either because he is looking down or the mousy brown waves cupping his face have melded to his forehead and hood them. He looks like he's spent a lifetime living on the darker side of inside and his pallid face is bleached of any natural hue. He finds his way to his bench. I can see his trousers peeking from below his gown; they are hanging limp and formless. They are a dull, dead brown. So are his shoes.

He takes his seat.

The magistrate nods – at no one in particular.

Sandra shuffles her papers beside me. She stands, hoists her gown from her shoulders and pulls it closed in the middle.

Only then does she read the charges out loud.

The magistrate leans forward from behind his high bench, his face even chalkier.

"You heard the charges against you?" he asks the accused.

"Yes."

"The first charge is one of malicious damage to property. Do you understand the charges against you? What do you plead?"

"Not guilty."

He is opposite me, just a few metres away in the accused's box, almost within reach, with his feet spread wide and hips locked forward. His head is back and his chin lifted high; his neck extends like a thick, hardened rope, flexed tight. His sleeves are pulled taut over his arms as he holds them behind him. It looks as though his hands are cuffed. They aren't.

His mouth is open, his lips parted. They are hanging slack and cruel.

He's ugly.

There is a clock on the wall behind him. It is round and white, edged with silver. It seems incongruous in that time-worn teak interior: too new and too shiny, an afterthought, as if too many have asked, "How much longer?"

The hands move round and round.

It is 09:17.

"The second charge is assault with intent to do grievous bodily harm. Do you understand that charge?" the magistrate continues mildly.

"Yes."

"What do you plead?"

"Not guilty."

Nineteen

"When you went to the police station and made the first statement, do you agree that you lied?"

"I lied," I admit.

It is the defence advocate's very first question to me about my testimony. He is placing up front, on the record of his cross-examination, that I am a confirmed liar.

"Why did you lie?"

"Because the accused threatened to kill me and my child," I say, my mind replaying the image of him running his hand across his throat, his words running cold down my neck: "… and you have a child."

I remember how he had grinned, an icy sneer across his face.

"Is that the only reason you lied?" asks the defence, his tone suggesting otherwise.

"I lied out of fear. His last words to me when he left my house that morning were 'I am going to fuck you over'."

"Did you not lie so that you can make an insurance claim?"

"No, I never lied because I could make an insurance claim. They would have paid out anyway if I told the truth."

I lied because I was terrified.

I am going to fuck you over.

It had been light by the time he eventually left that Sunday morning. I had listened from my room as he stalked up and down my passage, repeatedly calling his employee to fetch him. Only once he slammed the door and kicked my dog did I trust that he truly was gone.

A sleepless night being held hostage by him and his violent unpredictability had left me overwhelmed with fear. Having his hands hard around my throat, choking me, robbing me of any power I had over my next breath – the underlying threat that he could kill me when he chose – had left me paralysed and uncertain of what to do next.

It had been late Sunday afternoon, about 16:00, before I finally found the courage to open my door and drive to the police station to make a statement and get a case number. I wrote how I'd carelessly left my handbrake down and that my car had rolled into the wall. It was a weak statement and it wouldn't have held scrutiny, but his threats hung heavy in my mind, his finger marks lingered on my neck, and I was not going to challenge him.

In the end I'd never claimed from the insurance company. He had offered to pay for the repairs to my car during one of his endless phone calls when he apologised, cajoled, charmed and drew me in as he committed himself to making amends. But he never did honour his undertaking and in the end I had paid.

But I was uncomfortable not having told the truth.

Immediately after my radio show, on the Monday morning, I had made my way back to the police station. I met with the superintendent. I told him all that had happened. I showed him the bruises on my neck. I showed him the marks down my arms.

I told him I lied.

I told him why I lied and I asked his advice.

"Tell the truth," he said. "Change your statement, but I suggest you also get a restraining order. Although, I must warn you that, in my experience, this is only the beginning," he had said earnestly, the morning sun clouding behind him.

So I changed my statement.

I tell the court all of this.

I tell how I had made one statement about the car to the police and another to the Family Court for the restraining order.

I have already testified about the night of the Janet Jackson album launch at Insomnia nightclub. Sandra put her questions to me when she led my testimony and I have shared the details of how he drove through the streets of Parkhurst like a maniac, screaming, "Tonight you're going to die". I told how he dragged me through my house, how he swore at me and throttled me and kept me up all through the night. I have explained how I was so afraid.

But my details fall short of what really happened.

I have not told how I thought I was going to die.

I have not told how I thought I'd never see my son again.

How I did everything to stay alive.

How can I even begin to explain my fear? Words are useless as I sit there in the courtroom with him so close and me reliving my terror. There is no way to begin telling. Besides, no one asks.

Sandra asks me how I felt and I respond that I was afraid; but it was so much more than simple fear – but to tell all of that I would need a direct question: "Did you think you were going to die?"

Then I would say, "Yes."

Yes, I thought I was going to die.

But otherwise I will never utter those words.

I can't bring myself to announce to the world how close I have come to dying. I am too afraid to acknowledge it, even to myself.

And I am ashamed, ashamed that it has happened to me and that I was unable to stop it or defend myself. As a child, I had vowed to myself – and over the years I have repeated it silently, the same words, again and again – that *It will never happen to me. I will never be beaten up. Never. Ever ...*

I have broken my own promise.

But I also don't want him to have those words, to take ownership of them. I don't want him to know that he defeated me – and so utterly. I don't want him to know that he'd won. If I breathe those words, with him stretched out in the accused's box a few quick steps away, he'll know how terrified I really was that night, and even worse, he'll know that I'd always be scared.

So I tell the court that I lied because I was afraid.

But it isn't enough.

The defence wants my complete annihilation. He hacks away at me for many more hours, backwards and forwards, this way and that, repeating himself over and over, relentlessly swinging his verbal axe as though I am a liar, a cheat and a fraud.

"So when you went and made the false statement for insurance purposes, that was your personal decision?" he prods again, pausing briefly as if struggling to reconcile my *abhorrent* behaviour with his moral outrage. "A back-up plan to possibly put in an insurance claim for the damages is that correct?"

"At that point, yes," I repeat.

"And you knew at the time you were lying?"

"Yes, I knew I was lying."

"And you have no objection to taking the oath?"

"I did have an objection – which is why I went the next morning to change my statement."

"Madam, at the time that you did it, you had no objection?"

"I was afraid."

"It is a simple yes-or-no answer … You had no objection to taking the oath?" he sighs, as if nothing is more tedious than me being a perjurer.

"I took the oath," I say.

"Without objection?"

"Without objection."

Then it is lunch.

⊙

There is only one other place to eat aside from the court canteen. It is a tearoom disguised as a restaurant on the other side of Fox Street.

Inside it is dark; the only light filtering through is from windows tinted in once-shiny silver. The tables are crowded together and most are already crammed with lawyers when we arrive, all of them with their heads close together in collegial discussion or otherwise consulting urgently with their clients.

It seems there is much to accomplish in that one hour over lunch.

We take a table furthest from where the accused and his defence team are holding counsel between mouthfuls of bad food.

I turn my back to them as my mother, Sheryl and my friends gather around me.

Our toasted cheese sandwiches arrive. They are limp and greasy, with no garnish to redeem them.

It is impossible to eat.

I sit there collecting my thoughts. I've been testifying for three-and-a-half hours already and still have a long afternoon ahead.

We arrive back at court to find Sandra frantically searching for me.

"There's a problem," she announces, her glossed lips tight.

They are not words I want to hear.

"What problem?"

"The media want to publish the photographs."

"What photographs?" I ask, hoping I have misunderstood.

"The photos of you, beaten up."

"They can't. I won't let them."

I am firm as I stand my ground.

"Sorry, there's nothing you can do," she says, stroking my arm gently. "They've been entered into the court records as evidence, which means they're now in the public domain."

Her words hit me hard as I absorb their punches, their implication.

Thoughts of pictures of my battered face being made public crowd me as I take my seat and continue under oath.

"In your statement, in terms of the Domestic Violence Act, did you mention the two cars that you mentioned in your testimony, as being in the vicinity of the accused and yourself, when there was a change in driver of your vehicle, on your version?" asks the defence as though we hadn't taken a breath since my closing words before lunch.

I think carefully to make sense of his convoluted question.

What is he actually asking?

I testified earlier about two cars stopping as I was running away down the road, after he'd pulled up the handbrake and the car had swerved to a standstill. The drivers of those cars had shouted through their windows, asking whether I needed help. I have told the court how humiliated I was, stumbling down the middle of the road with my sleeve torn from my jacket, but I've also explained that despite my bewilderment and shame and fear, the accused had possession of my car, my car keys and my house keys and that I had felt I had no other option but to get back into my vehicle with him.

Now he is asking me whether I mentioned the two cars in my application for the restraining order. No I hadn't. It wasn't a necessary detail.

"I made no mention of the two cars, no."

"Any reason why not?"

"I made no mention of him pulling me out of my car or pulling up the handbrake either; I'm afraid there were too many events to condense into a few lines."

"Did anyone compel you to condense your version to a few lines?" he taunts.

"No, I filled up the piece of paper."

I had stood for hours in a queue at the Family Court to seek an interdict against him, stood among women who, in desperation, were turning to the court as a last resort for protection. I had summarised and filled the page with a description of the events that took place in my home. I had not included all the details of the journey home. I didn't think they were necessary – just as I didn't think what happened through the night, being choked and strangled, was needed for the insurance company.

The defence is now suggesting that these two statements are contradictory and cannot possibly be true. He moves swiftly on to the accused's version.

"He denies having assaulted you in any way or verbally abusing you for the alleged nine and a half hours that you claim."

"He is lying."

"He says that you are lying in your testimony and this is evidenced by the fact that you previously lied when you made your statement, which you refer to as being for insurance purposes."

"I am sorry, what are you asking me?"

"He says that you are lying. You keep saying that he is lying. He says you are lying and this was evidenced by the fact you made a false statement albeit, as you say, for insurance purposes.'"

"I am sorry ... I'm not quite with you."

The defence then takes my story and makes it theirs.

Every allegation I have made takes on their version.

If I have told how he was screaming at me, they invert it and claim that I was the one screaming at him.

It goes on endlessly.

Later, the defence vehemently denies that the accused had a drug problem – instead, he suggests that I had one, that I had a Prozac and Valium dependency.

They are shameful allegations. They are reckless and false, with no regard for their destructive impact.

And no one stops them.

I sit alone.

Twenty

I'm on the floor, the mottled pink Marley tiles cold to the touch beneath me. My hands clasp the toilet bowl while I vomit, my stomach churning as I spew my tension.

My mother and Sheryl wait in the passage outside the prosecutor's bathroom.

My forehead is clammy as I rest my head on the black toilet seat, allowing the waves of nausea to shudder through me. My knees are drawn in close, my heels hard against the filthy floor. I curl myself up smaller, hold the veined, porcelain toilet bowl tighter as the prospect of the hours ahead rage through my mind.

Today is the second day I'm under oath, defending myself and fending off a carefully calculated narrative. Yesterday I heard how I lunged at him with a serrated knife, one that had apparently been lying on my server at the front door. I tried to hold myself together, stay composed, as I fielded the endless allegations. I struggled to neutralise my expression, to hold my face vacant, as horrendous images were conjured up in the courtroom, but it was difficult to keep the horror from my eyes. I had tried to pretend that the defence advocate was talking about someone else, not me.

Because he wasn't talking about me.

I had never been in *a frenzy*, as purported. I had never tried to stab him. There had never been a knife. I had never aimed a sliver of glass at his naked foot. His feet were not without shoes.

It was all untrue.

When I had heard time and again how he defended himself, how his elbow had accidently struck my eye and the back of my head hit the wall, I wanted to howl my pain. I wanted to leap from my seat, to rush at the defence, to glower deep into his small, swollen eyes, and wail my anguish.

How can you do this?

Do you have no shame?

Where is your compassion?

But I couldn't. Not simply because I would never do such a thing. I had had to sit there and look calm and show the very least emotion lest I added another stroke to the abhorrent picture they were painting of me as a liar, a cheat, a fraud, a woman who is neurotic, obsessive and mentally ill, with a prescription drug dependency. A bad mother.

Theirs is a plot I had anticipated, but it had exploded beyond rigorous scrutiny. A further violation.

I felt as though I was being brutalised all over again in that courtroom; my attacker – the defence advocate, under the instruction of the attorney.

I don't consider for a minute that he believes his client is being honest or that his story is true. But it doesn't seem to matter, factual guilt or innocence is irrelevant, it is simply a costly game of winning: a tactical, vigorous play of catch, circle, strike, and then mercilessly pick the carcass clean, victoriously.

I am his carrion.

And he is going to pluck my bones bare.

Minutes pass. I finally scrape myself off the floor, flush the toilet and wipe my mouth. I am both sweaty and cold as I move to the basin. I lean against the wooden table with its skinny legs. Someone has covered it with a crocheted doily tablecloth. There is a wilting flower in a small ceramic vase placed to the side. Alongside it is a pink, quilted tissue box.

I pull tissues out and dab at the damp on my face. I smooth the smudged mascara from under my eyes. Check myself in the mirror.

I am drained and pale; the only hint of colour is my outfit. I am wearing buttercup yellow from top to toe.

God forbid, who wears yellow?

But it is my armour of courage.

My mother and Sheryl stay close to me as we make our way down the passage.

The defence team is already knotted together as I step into the courtroom; the defence advocate – new to the bar, yet to represent alleged drug traffickers and mobsters, and corruption-accused politicians – is waiting, and alongside him is the attorney with his black jacket sagging sloppily from his shoulders, his thin black tie dangling like a serpent around his neck. He stands tall, with his raven-black hair tied at the nape of his neck. It is hanging thick and greasy down his back. I want to rub the slick from my hands as his black eyes dart over me.

Together they are priming themselves, getting ready to prove their adversarial worth.

Neither of them greets me.

The accused is loitering beside them, hands in pockets.

Sandra looks up from her papers as I move closer.

"How are you feeling?" she asks.

"Not good."

"Don't worry, everything is going to be okay," she says.

She is smiling warmly but her now-familiar words already offer little comfort.

○

"The accused tells me, based on the tempestuous relationship the two of you had … you were obsessed with your job and your public image. Do you have any comment?"

"Well, I take my career seriously," I say guardedly. "Obsessed is a bit extreme."

I wonder what my career has to do with him beating me up but it soon becomes evident. It seems my moods fluctuate in accordance with the amount of work I have, and apparently if I don't have work I am snappy, irrational and on edge.

I have been on the stand for over an hour already.

The morning session had started late after the defence advocate requested a delay so that he could attend a scheduled meeting at the Attorney-General's office. It seems he is an important man. He's also had the impertinence to suggest, without any consultation, that it might suit me too as it means I could wrap up my radio show without having to rush out before the end to get to court on time. Perhaps he wants us all to think that not only is he in the big league and busy, but he is considerate too.

Now he stands, flushed with prominence, after I'm sworn in again. He runs his hands through his thinning blond hair, his puffy eyes looking forward, his nose planing into his pointed profile when he throws his first barb.

"Miss Going, yesterday we dealt with the issue of credibility and you told this court that you wouldn't exaggerate your testimony. Do you remember that?"

Of course I remember that.

"Do you still stand by that?"

I am confident that I haven't exaggerated my testimony and respond accordingly.

But the suggestion is already dangling ominously in the air.

I am acutely aware of the enthralled stares of the journalists seated on the hard wooden benches along the back of the courtroom.

Their pens are poised. They are ready to start scribbling.

I'd read their stories in the daily newspapers delivered casually to the studio this morning. I'd turned them open quickly, flicking through the pages, tossing them aside like they might catch fire, in my search for yesterday's torment.

I will buy none of their papers this weekend.

I will only see the articles years later, when Sheryl hands over my legal files. They are all there. My battered face, my fractured words, his despicable allegations printed in black and white, saved for posterity, in the *Saturday Star*, *Die Beeld*, *The Citizen*, the *Sunday Times* and who knows where else.

The journalists are waiting for their story to unfold.

Once the defence advocate is certain of rapt attention, he boldly places on record that my testimony was motivated by a desire to take money from the accused.

My testimony is motivated by a desire to take money from the accused.

I am going through this ordeal for money?

This, coming on behalf of a man who'd beaten me up then rushed back inside as my neighbour and his son were dragging me out, pulling me through the wooden shards of my exterior door, to steal money I had lying around in an envelope. I had turned to see him enter my home. It was then that he had stolen it.

I want to be sick again.

How dare they?

It seems that if the defence team can't silence me, then they will make sure that I am not heard.

And if that isn't enough I am now being indicted for having a poor self-image.

"Can I put it to you bluntly …? Your moods are determined by your self-esteem, which in turn is determined by how busy you were in your work …" I never heard the remainder of his words.

Bluntly?

"You can put it to me bluntly," I snap. "And I will tell you that I was extremely busy during that time and if my moods depended on how busy I was and my self-esteem, then I had very good self-esteem at that stage."

He pauses for as long as I speak, and then continues tonelessly.

"And he says that this is also evidenced from your testimony … when you said that he took a shard of glass … which is denied … that he wanted to ruin your career by damaging your face …"

I remember how I'd broken free and run when I felt the razor edge of the glass on my face, his spit on my cheek.

I remember how I wouldn't let him cut my face.

"He took a shard of glass and he was trying to cut my face," I say. My words are clipped and clear. "He said to me, 'You need your fucking face, don't you?' It was very deliberate."

"That is denied," he scoffs. "He says it is indicative of the way you believe that everything went together with your work ... the self-esteem ... your face ... your image ... Everything was this public personality, the *image* that you had."

"What are you asking me?" I ask slowly and deliberately.

"I'm *explaining* to you what the accused's instructions are."

"I don't understand ... Must I comment on what the accused believes?"

"Yes. I've invited you to comment," he says, as though it is obvious to all. "The accused *says*, not *believes* ..." he continues, "that you perceived this whole fight and all these incidents to be related to your work ... and that you saw everything in relation to your work. You are obsessed with this public image that you have!"

I breathe in deep, lift my chin, and only then do I answer.

"Bruises on my face and eyes closed swollen, I believe are related to my work. Yes."

Twenty-one

"Now in your evidence, and that statement," he says, flicking his pale hand at an imagined sheet of paper, "you say, and I quote: 'He was continuously kicking me all over my body.' Do you remember that?"

How will I ever forget?

"Yes, and he was," I say.

"I have instructions to put it to you that if that was the case … you would have marks on your body, which do not appear in the doctor's report," he announces loudly.

As the smugness slips from the defence advocate's mouth I instinctively put my arms around my stomach and hold myself safe.

I remember how I cowered into a ball and rocked on the ground, in forced rhythm with each of his deliberate, running kicks. His grunts of exertion are loud in my memory, rumbling in my head as he heaves himself backwards and forwards trying to inflict the most damage, with my dog, Garp, muffling my screams with frenzied, warm, wet licks. I remember how glad I was that he wasn't wearing his sturdy, leather boots.

As the defence denies yet again that his client was wearing shoes, my eyes are drawn to his feet. I will turn to look at them every time I hear this denial. I can't help myself. As I look at him now his legs are crossed and he is leaning forward. He is resting his elbows on his thighs, his right foot jerking furiously. It is like a red-hot flare fighting its predetermined trajectory, like a beacon begging attention in its disavowal. He is wearing the very same brown suede shoes.

I turn my attention from his shoes as the defence advocate pushes toward me, waving the J88 medical forms about. It is being presented as hard, documented evidence that no bruises were recorded on my torso. It is a visual castigation and he is delighted to be brandishing it about.

"And I put it to you that there are no injuries recorded for anywhere on your body other than your face and head," he says, pushing a copy into my hand.

"Yes ... my primary injuries were from my shoulders up," I agree.

"Do you see anywhere on this report that it is restricted to *primary* injuries?" he sneers.

"At no point was I asked to take my clothes off to check for bruising on my body ... I had such pain in my head. I was not concerned about the bruises on my ribs."

The image is with me as I speak. I am lying on a bed in the hospital ward. I am clutching my eye and I'm crying. I'm trying not to sob. Dr McKenzie is prodding and poking me with gentle hands, trying to establish the extent of my wounds, when I elbow her away and tug my T-shirt down.

It is yet another physical invasion and I don't want it.

I don't want to be touched.

"Don't worry about my back," I mumble. "It's my eye ... Please do something about the pain in my eye."

But the court apparently needs more.

The defence advocate proceeds to read the district surgeon's statement out loud.

"Madam, do you see what paragraph 7 says ...?"

"Yes."

"Paragraph 8, 'condition of clothing: intact with some blood stains'."

"Yes."

"Paragraph 9, 'state of the person: physical powers, general state of health and mental state'. What is the doctor's comment there?" he asks loudly.

"Stable. I am in stable mind."

I am glad to be saying those words. The words roll off my tongue. I know what Dr McKenzie means, but I fleetingly appreciate another interpretation. I am in stable mind. I want to hold onto the phrase, but the defence advocate moves swiftly on.

"It says that you were stable – and you agree that there is no indication of any bruises or injuries anywhere on your body that would be consistent with being kicked all over the body."

"Yes. I never reported them to her."

"Any reason you chose not to?"

"Because I was more concerned with the pain in my head," I say again.

He continues with his line of questioning, again accusing me of exaggerating my injuries in order to claim financially from his client.

"Because what I am putting to you, Madam, and you don't seem to be answering, is that this is indicative of exaggeration on your part. It was never an issue before. You never mentioned it before and on our version it never happened before," he announces, pausing for effect. "And now, months after the incident, you are referring to things that you never referred to in any statement or any letter or even to a doctor in a clinical examination."

"I am sorry, what did I not refer to?" I ask, confused.

"To bodily injuries."

"In my statement I said that he was kicking me. That is bodily injuries."

The courtroom is quiet.

I don't look around. I stare straight ahead.

"Madam ... I am putting to you and it is the basis of my cross-examination that you are exaggerating."

And still he moves on. He goes on to refute my allegation that the marks on my face are shoeprints.

I listen and I answer, but I'm getting tired. I feel it in my slouching shoulders, the constant banging in the back of my head, in my limp hands folded in my lap.

It is almost lunchtime.

I try not to think that the day is not even half over.

I concentrate to hear his words.

"I infer from your previous statement that Dr McKenzie is actually a female. It is a lady who examined you?"

"That is right. A lady," I say.

"So there was no reason on your part not to show her any injuries on your body. Is that correct?" he asks.

Yes, he is correct, but I am having none of it. Again I feel the anger welling up inside me, breaking through the fatigue.

"If the basis of your cross-examination is exaggeration, then I can assure you I would have exaggerated and I would have documented all sorts of marks that weren't there," I say, looking straight at him.

"With respect, that is precisely what you are saying there," he says looking at the magistrate, ignoring me.

"No. I never made any mention of the bruises on my body," I say forcefully. "I underplayed the damage inflicted on me."

I can just see Sheryl out of the corner of my eye. I see her fine curls flouncing around her as she firmly nods her approval. I don't need to look to know that she is smiling.

But her movement draws attention and soon everyone becomes restless.

The defence takes the opportunity to gather together the photographs that have been submitted by me as evidence. They are stacked one upon the other, burnished images of destruction; my garage, my lounge, me. He holds them up, away from him, as though they might tarnish his hand, before throwing his next question across the courtroom.

"Is there any reason why you sought to have *these* blown up to the size of A4?"

His words crush me.

The red rises in my cheeks.

Shame comes over me in a rush as he belittles me and my printed evidence.

I can feel the magistrate's eyes on me.

He too wants to know why I have enlarged the pictures to foolscap.

"I think for very obvious reasons. They are evidence of what your client did to me," I say slowly, trying not to look at the images in the grip of the defence advocate's hand.

It is the picture on top that distresses me most. It is me.

He is flaunting my face. He is denting the paper as he holds it forward, scornfully, dismissing me in my pain.

I know the picture well.

The deep shadow cast behind me frames my face where my eye has been battered shut, my lashes are knitted together in seeping ooze. My other eye stares ahead. I am marbled in red, purple, black and blue.

The photograph was taken a few days after he beat me.

"I put it to you that it is further indicative of the fact that you wish to exaggerate your evidence and to highlight that which suits you." He is looking at the magistrate as he erases me, reinforcing his viewpoint that I am not worthy of even a glance. "Do you have any comment?"

I really don't want to comment.

I just want it all to be over.

But it isn't – it continues for some time.

I almost don't hear the magistrate when he finally adjourns for lunch.

"We can adjourn," he says, his three words sounding as one.

This time, my mother, Sheryl, my friends and I avoid the restaurant in Fox Street and instead wend our way to the court canteen. None of us wants to fortify ourselves with the defence team only a table or two away. Yesterday was enough.

We make our way upstairs, away from the criminal courts with their dusty stairways leading down to basement cells. We step out onto the concourse. The walls are impressively clad in cold, cream-coloured terrazzo. The floor is grey stone, its brittleness long since polished away. It extends high and wide, enough for two double-decker buses to pass each other. There are signs hanging tiredly.

They have lost their whiteness. They are warped with green borders and headings but they show us where to go. Four floors up.

To reach the lift, we move past the marble columns threaded with gold and black. They dwarf the corridors with their gilded tapestry of complexity, like truth intertwined with lies and deception.

The lift doors open into a canteen that is government standard, uninviting.

I order a plate of chips knowing I can't eat.

My food arrives like a tangle of pale, pulpy limbs slithering in their own grease. They are like the appendages that will slide over the phone records for the rest of the day.

"Miss Going, my client says that you testified that you traced the call and you traced it back to the accused. Do you remember saying that?" asks the defence advocate, picking up on where we left off before lunch.

He is speaking of the call I received from Detective Potgieter many months earlier. I had given the details in my testimony with Sandra the day before.

"I did not say I traced it back to the accused."

"So, in other words it was incorrect to suggest that he was behind the call?"

"I would say it was a foregone conclusion that he was behind the call," I state confidently.

The accused is scratching at his notes again. He cannot sit quietly. He continuously drags his fingers through his hair and thrusts his fringe back. I don't want to look at him, but he is difficult to ignore. He is constantly shifting around, his jaw moving furiously; he snarls and smirks and snorts, while I contend and fend his exhaustive allegations and denials.

He passes the paper forward, his pen clicking violently.

The defence advocate reads it quickly.

"You saw I received a note from the accused? Who was the call traced back to?"

It is a brave question and I cannot wait to answer.

"It is an unlisted number," I announce clearly. "It is the same policeman that took his statement."

Detective Potgieter had taken the accused's statement the same day he pretended to be a reporter with the late-night 'Dr Jekyll Mr Hyde' phone call. He had signed his name as the attending officer as the accused detailed how he had lifted his arm in self-defence and how his elbow had accidentally hit my eye.

"Who is this? What is the policeman's name?" enquires the magistrate.

I'm surprised to hear his thin, reedy voice and am quite taken aback that he is finally asking a question that might favour me.

"Detective Potgieter," I announce and then continue garrulously. "He has always referred to him as 'Pottie', and I think he has been promoted to superintendent."

The defence doesn't flinch.

"As I have put it to you, my client denies any involvement in this telephone call. Any comment?" he asks.

"I cannot comment on him denying it."

And I really can't.

Twenty-two

"Mommy, I drew you a picture," he yells.

And in that moment, as his words soar across the schoolyard, suddenly nothing else matters. Seeing his grey socks around his ankles and his black shoes chafing at the ground as he rushes toward me are enough to hold back the past. As he picks up speed I watch his shirt escaping the confines of too-long shorts flapping around knobbly knees.

I wanted to shout, "Jelly Tots."

Those are his words always: "Mommy, I love you lots and lots like Jelly Tots."

As I stand excitedly behind the high wire fence waiting for him to break through the open gate, it is as though my heart is a melted, glistening mass of bright gelatine. It is squidgy and hot and sticky.

His smile is big and broad and toothless, his two front teeth newly missing. His eyes are crinkled closed and disappear into a face, scrunched and smiling, beneath a head of light, blond hair bleached even whiter in the shining, midday sun.

It is beautiful to see my child lost in such glee, such happiness.

He seems to have settled into Grade 1 nicely and appears to be coping well with the fact that his father is now living overseas – although he still has those inevitable moments when he is withdrawn and quiet and prefers to be alone, or otherwise insists on having me close by and within his sights. But, as the child psychologist assures me, it is acceptable behaviour given the trauma he's had to endure.

For now, as I watch him through the diamond shapes of the fence, he is a blithe six-year-old accelerating toward his mother after an exhausting morning at big school. His small, pudgy hand is clasping a huge sheet of paper. It is almost as big as him and is billowing and crackling like a large, white sail as he approaches me.

"Look, Mom, it's you!" he calls, pleased.

"Oh, that's wonderful," I squeal.

I snatch the picture away with child-like enthusiasm.

"Let me see," I say breathlessly.

It is me in stick form. My arms are open wide. I had five straight fingers on each hand. My head is an enormous circle and my smile red and wide. I have two eyes. The one a crisp, cobalt, crayon blue. The other a scratched-out, dark hole staring back at me like a damning blot of blackness.

The hot, dry air fills the last of my laugh.

Oh my god!

My child!

What have I done!

I stare at the picture.

"That's lovely," I say quickly, my smile locked to my face. "Let's go," I continue, before we turn the corner and walk the one block home.

As I tuck the picture beneath my arm, I take his hand. I try to hold it loose between my fingers so that he knows nothing of the tightness within me. His drawing has seared my soul. To be reminded that his innocence, his purity and his wholeness are forever gone is a heavy burden for a mother. This is further proof of how deeply he has been affected. I know there is nothing I can do to change it and I accept that I have to let his fear, his confusion and his pain rise to the surface. I have to allow him his hurt.

And I am the one who has brought it upon him.

It is me who has passed on the violence.

I had never considered for a moment, when moulding my own

life, that I would ever fall victim to any form of abuse, and I had most definitely never foreseen it for my child. I have only ever wanted him to grow up sure, safe and confident. He is a gentle child. An only child. He has never learnt to fight, not even with a toy gun. I wouldn't allow him to have one. I will have nothing in my home that suggests anger and hatred in any form, and somehow, in some unfathomable way, I've allowed the violence in.

I have to accept that this is in him now and it will always be between us.

As I keep him slightly separate from my side, I know I have to let it be. I have to leave space for the ineludible sting of having invited violence into his life. It is a sting that will arrive unbeckoned, even in times of safety, hidden in innocent and colourful artwork.

When we get home I place the picture at the back of a cupboard. Soon I will throw it away. I don't want it lying around. I don't want to come upon it unexpectedly, and I most definitely don't want my son to happen upon it unnecessarily and be reminded of me, his mother, being battered.

It is not right to see your mother broken. It is not the natural order of the world. It is not meant to be.

I want to be unbroken – for him. I want to stand before him brave and strong, otherwise how will he ever be able to trust me to protect him and keep him safe if I was unable to defend even myself, or to keep myself whole.

I am his mother. I carried him in my womb.

He is from me and of me. I am in him, he in me.

It will be my actions that flash as visual cues through his life. It will be my voice in his head when he tries to make sense of the world. It will be me who allows him his birth right, that he be protected, loved and nurtured.

I want him to confidently take his place in the world and it is me that should let him know that he is deserving of it. It should be me who leads the way. However, in order for me to do that I need to know where I, myself, am meant to be. I have left my childhood behind and for much of my adult life I have focused on making another existence for myself. I had reached a point where

I considered myself worthy. I had found and taken my place and I had believed that where I was standing and where I was going was nothing less than absolute and defined. But the day I was beaten up was the day I was robbed of my certainty.

I know I need to reclaim my sense of self, my being, my value and my importance so that I can heal and, in so doing, engage completely with my son. And the most immediate way to do so is through the court case.

But I hadn't thought it would be the way it is. I hadn't expected not to be believed. I hadn't anticipated being disregarded, ignored and belittled. I had proceeded with legal action trusting that all would be fine; that the court is about upholding the law and that justice is much more than incidental. I had naively thought that power and privilege know their place.

So although I still believed, more than ever, that what I was doing was necessary and right, especially for my son, I can't pronounce with certainty that I would have laid charges if I'd had any understanding of the tirade of abuse that lay ahead.

The court case had been remanded to 9 and 10 June. It was another three very long months away. Eight months had already passed since he had beaten me up. I had already spent two gruelling days on the stand testifying. I know there is more to come.

It is me who has been put on trial. I am the one they find either guilty or innocent.

But, aside from the systematic, attempted destruction of me as a person and a mother in the courtroom, now my battered face is being splashed over newspapers and magazines countrywide.

Then there is the Domestic Violence Bill of 1998. It is being amended and somehow, in between the re-writing and the broadening of the definition of domestic violence, my once-unsullied name has becoming synonymous with women abuse.

I can't go anywhere without being recognised. I see people elbowing each other as I pass them, nudging each other urgently as they whisper loudly.

"It's her."

"Who?"

"The one who got beaten up."

"Who?"

I see a hand being lifted, cupped to a mouth in disbelief, and an eyebrow raised. I notice the knowing nods.

"Oh, that one!"

"Yes … Shame."

I avert my eyes, and quicken and lighten my step as I pretend not to hear, not to see.

I am being inundated with correspondence at work. I am receiving letters and faxes and, as much as I appreciate the words of solace, comfort, consolation, I find myself unable to respond.

I am being detained in public as other women open their wounds and share their own brutal stories with me.

One mid-week afternoon I am at the local supermarket, still hesitant to venture far from my home. I am standing at the fresh-meat counter alongside the fridges. The smell of chilling blood assails me when a woman, a little younger than me, approaches. She is pretty, with a broad, clean face, her complexion a warm, tawny brown. Her crimped black hair is pulled away from her face. I only notice because she calls my name.

"Tracy, it's you," she says with familiarity.

I look up, not sure whether I know her or not. She must see the confusion in my eyes.

"You don't know me, but I want to say thank you."

Then she introduces herself and, as she tells me her story, it is as though the torturous words spilling from her mouth are finally being set free. She has been silent for too long.

She had been married for several years and been abused for equally as many. She knew it was time to leave when she was knocked unconscious and came round to find her husband biting chunks of flesh from her back. She lifts her blue T-shirt and shows me her scars. They are like puckered wounds of mangled fibrosis. They have left their mark like violent sucks of depravity. I want to be sick. I want to run from the cold aisle and hurl my horror, but instead I find the strength to stand still and hold her tight as the tears silently drop from her lashes.

Only once I am back in my car do my thin walls collapse. It is then that I put my head down and allow the sobs to rip through me.

It is unimaginable the lives that so many women are living.

And, realistically, I am one of the lucky ones.

It is another day that I am at the same supermarket, this time at the till, when there is a gentle tap on my shoulder. It is a middle-aged man and he is holding a bunch of flowers. A mixed bouquet of yellow and white chrysanthemums, bright roses and green leaves.

"These are for you," he smiles warmly. "Everything will turn out fine for you, and you'll get over this thing."

He is gone before I can thank him.

I take comfort from his words and reassurance from his gentleness.

But I know that if I am being approached, being constantly reminded, then so too is my son. It is a blind deceit, self-deception, to hope that his friends aren't talking about it at school. They are.

He, too, will not be allowed to forget.

Then there are the nightmares. He has been having bad dreams for a while.

"Last night I dreamt he was here, Mom."

"It's okay, my boy," I say, tousling his rumpled hair. "Everything's going be okay."

"But, Mommy ..."

"It's only a dream."

The child psychologist has assured me that this, too, is very normal. But as I struggle to manage the chaos around me, there are many occasions when I wonder, what is truly normal? It seems to me that there is nothing much that is ordinary and usual.

Then, with his little knuckles white and his fists clenched tight, he'd punch at the air.

"Mommy, one day when I'm big, I'm going to hit him.

"Like this ...

"And this ...

"And *this!*"

Once he is spent, I take his fists and cup them in my hands and then pull him toward me so that I can hold him tight. There isn't much else I can do to stave off his terror. It'll be years before there is peace to his nights. He is a quiet boy, affable, never one to talk much about his internal musings, and even now as I write this book and ask him how he feels, his words are always the same.

"Mom, I don't want to think about it," his voice deep and gruff.

And again I have to let him be.

But still I say it.

"I'm so sorry."

Twenty-three

He is gone. But still he is here. He will always be here. There will never be a time when he is not a part of my nightmares, but, as with all bad memories, they eventually fade over the years. However, back then, he shadows me in my waking life, follows me at night as he haunts and alters my unconscious. He changes form in the dark as I sleep. He becomes taller, more angular, his arms and legs even longer as he punches and kicks me. His ominous dreamt presence hangs over me like an over-used, dirty prison blanket and, as its greyness shrouds me, I am smothered by its coarseness. Then, as my breath is drawn from my body, suffocated, the violent images of him integrated and consolidated in my mind to tear through my awareness, I awaken. I drag him with me to the surface. I thrash around as I untangle myself from what is real and what is imagined. And, as I try to make sense of it all, the images play over and over again in my mind like a soundless, silent black-and-white movie trapped in its sprockets and caught in the revolving repetitions as the film negative clicks over loudly, whirs and splutters, desperate to escape its own machinations.

I lie still as my heart pounds. Just as I did as a child, behind the drawn curtains, waiting for my father to negotiate the driveway, then stumble from the car to the front door. I wait breathless. I take slow breaths to calm myself, all the time clutching my duvet close to me as I stave off damp shivers. It is impossible to go back to sleep and so my day begins disjointed and anxious.

Other times I have conversations with him in my head as I imagine him apologising. I don't want him back – I want him well away from me – but there are times I need to pull him close to pretend a regretful acknowledgement of his violation.

And in those desperate ruminations I have a voice. I can speak. It is always my voice though. Not his. He will forever remain silent.

But it is only in these illusory conversations that my voice is loud and clear. In my day-to-day conversations, my voice is often hoarse and phlegmy. I am constantly sick, with one throat infection after another. My body responding to the trauma, an extemporaneous response to my unrelenting fight to reclaim myself. The infections strike me down repeatedly and, thinking about it and analysing all that has transpired, it reminds me how I'd been sick so often as a child. A childhood plagued with ear infections. I was continually being dragged from one doctor to another highly qualified physician, another ear, nose and throat specialist, always in the pursuit of a medical solution to my constant inflammation. But, looking back, it was simply my body acting as a receptacle to the ill around me, its immunity compromised by me not being heard, or me not wanting to hear.

For most of my childhood I'd protected and defended my mother, my brother and my sister where I could. Otherwise I tried to block out the noise, sometimes putting my hands over my ears so I couldn't hear, then always drawing my thumb into my mouth as I sucked rhythmically for my safety, my tears falling noiselessly.

In a household of abuse, as a child I was mostly helpless, but as a woman who's been battered, I want to be heard.

And it is in the courtroom that I expect to have a voice.

The last court appearance leaves me reeling, mute and ravaged, as I am assaulted with the words and argument of the defence advocate, his strategy a repugnant legal reply to my terrifying experience.

The remainder of the last afternoon in court is consumed with analysing the phone calls between me and the accused. I had unbelievably accepted fifty-eight phone calls from him and it was an opportunity for the defence to 'prove' that I had been cooperating with him, that I was complicit.

It is hard for me to justify taking those calls. I had taken out a restraining order to keep him away. It stated quite clearly that he was not allowed to threaten me, nor enter my domain. Technically, there is nothing untoward about me having answered his ceaseless, frantic calls, but I am not oblivious – I knew it was in that 'grey' area that hovered between right and wrong – that it wasn't legally appropriate. What I didn't know then, however, was that he'd come back to beat me.

Of course, he should never have called me in the first place, but perhaps it had been part of his game plan all along as he once again reminded me exactly who had the power and, whether we had a relationship or not, it would be on his terms. He had the authority to make fifty-eight phone calls if he so decided, whether the courts permitted him or not.

"It's not worth the paper it's written on," he'd scoffed, referring to the interdict.

I had been surprised to see his number on the screen when he first called, one week after the sheriff of the court had delivered the interdict.

I hadn't answered.

Then he phoned again.

And again.

Finally, I'd responded.

He'd phoned to apologise, he said.

Although I was tormented by having come so close to death at his hand and couldn't clear my mind of the images of being dragged through my home, of being choked, of being held powerless, I needed to hear his words. It helped me make sense of my confusion. Perhaps if he could explain his behaviour, then I could understand. I needed to understand.

Then there were the flowers, the offer to pay for the repairs to my car and my garage, the gift of air tickets so that I could take my son on a healing holiday.

Suddenly it was no longer all about my loss, my longing and feeling lost.

It became easier to hear his voice.

But then he beat me up.

And, unbelievably, sitting in the courtroom with him spread out ominously a few metres away, I still want answers. I still want to know ... Why?

Why did he do it?

Why me?

Why had I allowed it?

Why hadn't I seen it?

The answers would only come over the years, and especially now, as I write. Back then, I was simply trying to survive. Then, getting much-needed help for me was an indulgence I couldn't afford. I didn't have the money, and besides, my son was more important and all my resources were going into lawyers, rebuilding our safety, and healing him. I took him to a child psychologist until she, herself, felt my son no longer needed the sessions. But with hindsight, I didn't have the strength back then. I didn't have the emotional grit to begin the arduous journey of exploring my past in an attempt to comprehend my present and future, and in so doing unpack the complexity of my own inheritance.

I did see a psychologist for a short while. Sheryl wanted a psychological report for the civil matter that was by now unfolding alongside the criminal case and it was on her recommendation that I saw Leonard.

Leonard is deeply religious and wore a yarmulke. I would meet with him in his home office, and as I sat on the couch opposite him I would hear his children playing in the garden, their light laughter tinkling through the open window.

On my second meeting with Leonard he told me he had originally been approached by the defence to provide a psychological justification for the accused, to be an 'expert' witness. Leonard had instantly and unhesitatingly declined. He was not interested. He had no intention of ever vindicating violence. He was a man, to me at least, of enormous integrity, one who had little tolerance for abusive behaviour.

I think he shared this detail of the defence's approach because he wanted to reassure me that he was on my side. He understood that I had been completely overwhelmed by all that had happened – and continued to happen – and also appreciated the might and means being thrown at defending the accused and keeping him out of jail. But I found it unnerving. I could never completely give my mind over to him and trust him. I was concerned that there was a part of him that might have believed the accused's version; perhaps it had already been put to him on that initial approach.

And, of course, he was a man. How could a man even begin to identify with what I'd been put through?

But when I watched Leonard giving his expert opinion on panel discussions between broadcasts from the courtroom of the Oscar Pistorius trial I realised that I could have – should have – trusted him completely. I had only stayed long enough for him to formulate an opinion on my state of mind and submit it as a report for my civil matter, and I'd never gone back. But watching his discerning response to all that had unfolded between Oscar and Reeva was evidence of his sound understanding of the power play between an abuser and his victim. In the months I spent watching the trial, Leonard appeared regularly, and I came to realise that he really did understand.

So, as I neared this chapter, I reached out to Leonard, but this time of my own volition.

Dear Leonard

I hope you don't mind me contacting you. I'm on the last stretch of my book and I'm writing about the court case now. I'm getting to the part where I take the accused's endless calls after him holding me hostage for an entire night and assaulting me – and me getting a restraining order.

Obviously, I look very stupid for taking all these calls – even after all these years I'm trying to understand why.

What is it about me (or anyone) that does that?

*I just remember always wanting to know why ... Why? Why?
I wanted him to say sorry. To say he didn't mean to do it.
It's complete madness.
But I would love to get some insight into it all.
Is it about worthlessness?
Thanks
Tracy*

Leonard's response was almost immediate.

*Hi Tracy
 I am so happy to hear from you.
 I often wonder how you are doing.
 These are not difficult questions.
 The clue to your question is: What were you trying to reclaim, that you felt bereft or robbed of; power, dignity, worth, etc.?
 The compulsion to keep going back is a desperate quest to reclaim those things, to beat the man at his game. It is a game he is diabolically good at – even when he appears to be losing, he is just using another well-practised ploy.
 Also the shame, self-blame and humiliation keep you desperately trying to get vindication, trying to turn things around so that you can make it right after all.
 Then there is the weird Stockholm Syndrome solidarity with the abuser, where you unconsciously tell yourself [that] if you prove yourself to him he will love and protect you the way he promised before something (in your own mind), maybe you, upset him and pushed him over the edge.
 These are some of the pointers off the top of my head.
 Let me know if I can be of further help.
 Warm wishes
 Leonard*

When I sent this letter to Leonard I had no intention of including either it or his response in these pages, but Leonard's words deeply affected me. Once again he had the insight to understand – except this time I would accept his astuteness trustingly and would share it gratefully.

He was right. I was trying to reclaim so much.

◯

But "Why? *Why?*" was a question I'd ask for many years.

I remember turning to my friend, Charlene, a highly respected journalist who was going through her own personal hell as she fought for survival through her own rape trial. She had come home one night to find a man hiding in her bathroom. He then raped her. He took her life and irrevocably changed it with his penis.

We were sitting outside the court waiting for the tea break to end before we all traipsed back into court. I was shattered, Charlene's comforting arm around me, when I looked up at her and said, "Can you believe it, but I still just want to know why? Why did he do this to me?"

She took me firmly by the shoulders, made me look her straight in the eyes.

"Don't expect an answer," she said. "He did it because he could … He did it because no one has ever stopped him."

She was right.

So, when tea was done, I stood up and walked back into the courtroom and I entered a little taller.

It was just the other day when my friend Estie, with her probing mind and intriguing way of thinking, who also spent many hours sitting on the hard, wooden benches supporting me in the courtroom, asked me a question.

"What would have happened if he had apologised?" she asked. "Would it have made any difference?"

It was a thought-provoking question, and it took me completely by surprise.

Would it have been enough, I wondered.

And, after much mulling, I have realised the answer is not without complexity.

Yes, an apology would have made an enormous difference to

me. It would have soothed some of my wounds and, if his words had been sincere and honest, it would have disarmed me of my overwhelming fear because he would no longer have been a personal threat.

But would it have made any difference to the process? Would it have meant that I would have decided against legal action? No, it would not. I was entitled to an apology, yes, but it wouldn't have absolved him of the consequences. It would perhaps have diluted my determination as I became less impassioned, less afraid, but there would always have been a need for retribution. It cannot be otherwise – there are consequences to hurtful, punishing actions.

So it was never going to be the one or the other. It would always be both.

But, of course, the irony is that it is probably he who would have benefitted the most by offering an apology. It would have been an opportunity for him to take cognisance of his conduct and take responsibility for his actions. It would have been a powerful deterrent for his future behaviour. But instead he would deny, lie, protest and defend and soon after he would go out and, unbelievably, beat up another woman.

God forbid.
Why?

But then of course I also had to look inward and ask *myself* why.

Why had I fallen for a man who was inherently violent and self-destructive?

What did that say about me?

I should have believed him when he first showed his true self, right in the early days, when I listened as he screamed at his ex-girlfriend on the phone.

"Leave me alone, you fucking bitch!" he'd shouted, each word matching a stride as he marched up and down my passage.

I remembered how he had stormed into the kitchen, his eyes still flashing in fury, his lips thin and tight, and how I'd exhaled slowly and only then commented, enunciating each word crisply and clearly, my message very clear.

"You wouldn't speak to me like that, would you?"

I recalled how he'd shrugged and, as the tension drained from his body, the words had tripped so casually from his tongue.

"I'd never do that to you," he'd said. "You'd never deserve it."

Then he smiled boyishly.

And I had believed him.

I knew I would never deserve it.

Those were the heady days when we were in love. It was the early phase of what I was convinced was a preordained relationship. He'd shared with me that his ex-girlfriend was unstable and irrational, and the one-sided conversation I'd overheard was proof enough. I knew I wasn't like her. I was sane and rational. And I knew I would never give him reason to be displeased; why would I? It was not in my nature to be so obtuse.

And, listening to his reassuring answer, it was obvious to me that I was 'the special one'. I was the right one for him.

Perhaps it was in that moment that I silenced my inner voice.

Maybe it was then, as I stood in my kitchen, accepting his abusive onslaught against another woman, that I made a near-deadly contract with my abuser.

It was possibly at that moment that I sealed my fate.

And him?

Was it then, as I stood quiet, and accepted his explanation, that he already knew I was next?

Was it when he uttered those chilling words, "You'd never deserve it," and transferred the responsibility of his future actions onto another, onto me, that he thought I'd be compliant?

Was it then, at that precise moment, that he knew that one day I would? That one day I *would* deserve it?

And if I didn't, he'd make absolutely, damned, bloody sure I did.

Twenty-four

"Does he have a new girlfriend?" I ask, taken aback.

"Who?" says Sandra, shuffling through her paperwork.

"Him," I say, raising my eyebrows, indicating across the courtroom.

We both turn and look.

He is standing at the defence table in his navy blazer, his white shirt, his chinos, and I can't see his shoes but I'd be surprised if he wasn't wearing his brown suede shoes. He is laughing loudly. I watch as he throws back his head and then brings his chin down to gaze into her eyes. He runs his hands through his hair.

She is right next to him, close to his side. I can only see her profile. She is also laughing, but it's more of a giggle. It is a coquettish, girly laugh. She leans toward him, almost touching him as she listens to what he has to say. Her hair is black-brown, thick and unruly as it sits loosely on her shoulders. Her face is unadorned. She is dressed in blue jeans and a casual shirt. It is a nondescript, comfortable outfit.

She is not what I considered his type. I am astonished, too, that he already has someone new in his life and, even more so, that she's accompanied him to court, especially given the circumstances, the accusation, the trial. I am quite incredulous of his brazenness.

I look at Sandra and shake my head.

She looks at me quizzically – then her words stop me.

"That's not his girlfriend. That's your new investigating officer."

"My new investigating officer?" I splutter.

"Yes," she chuckles.

"Since when do I have a new investigating officer?" I ask, my voice still squeaking.

"I don't know. But that's her. She introduced herself to me earlier."

She is still chuckling when she turns back to her papers.

And then I laugh. I laugh that Sandra is chuckling next to me, that she is able to chortle at my outrage. We both know it is a ridiculous outrage given the outrageousness of the outrageous matter we are battling. But it is very funny. It is also good to see her laugh. She is generous and kind and she's working hard to win this case, but I already know she doesn't stand a chance. In the beginning, I assumed the magistrate would factor in her youthful inexperience, but I have long ago come to the conclusion that he will not, that he will concede nothing, or very little, to her or to me.

When my laugh dies down I chuckle too.

I chuckle incredulously that he is flirting with my new investigating officer, that he feels the need to be irresistible and charming to her. It is unbelievable that he is so conniving and manipulative.

I chuckle at the irony that I have a new investigating officer, Investigating Officer No. 3, that she is a woman and she doesn't even introduce herself to me.

I can't believe it.

I'm still chuckling when I take my seat beside Sandra. It is the same maroon, fabric-covered chair I sit on every time. It is even dirtier.

Sometimes one can only laugh and chuckle. It is 08:55 and I am holding on to my spontaneity, that small joy, because it will come to an end the moment the magistrate slips through the door.

It is Tuesday, 9 June. Three days before my birthday. Almost a year since he escorted me to my birthday party, where I officially introduced him to all my family and friends. I had been so proud to present him to everyone then. But today there will be no pride.

Today I will again be shamed and I will wear that shame like a punishment for having allowed him into my life as I am ridiculed and derided for being a woman who fell in love with a man who did not exist.

My investigating officer takes her place on the hard, wooden benches.

I turn to look at the defence team. They are huddling together like a pack of laughing hyenas, set to cunningly catch their prey with their teeth, not their claws. The accused and his attorney are standing eye to eye. They both hunch their shoulders as they peer down at the defence advocate. Physically, he is not their predatory equal. He is considerably shorter and smaller, like the runt of the pack. Between their darkness, he is fair-haired. It is like the interplay between varying intensities of light; I know they are equally skilful as hunters and scavengers. I watch as they posture, plot and signal. They are readying themselves for the attack and, just like hyenas, there is nothing cowardly about them – they are bold and dangerous.

It is the third day straight that I will be their rotting flesh.

It is my last day on the stand, but I don't know that yet. As I sit next to Sandra, I have no idea how the day will unfold. But it will be my final day. Tomorrow Sandra will call on the district surgeon, then my sister, some friends and a journalist to whom the accused had warned: "If it wasn't for her child I would have gone ballistic on her" and "I have put a hit out on her".

Before she finally rests our case, Sandra will also call my neighbour.

My neighbour is not a man who likes to be exposed. He is an attorney himself but he is reticent by nature. He is slightly aggrieved that he has been called as a witness and it is clear that he'd rather be elsewhere than testifying in court. He will bear witness to my account of the attack. He will testify how his son heard me screaming and called to him, and how they both rushed to our shared wall to assist. As he recalls his version, sombre and expressionless, I will remember being on the ground as I was kicked. I will recall rocking in resistance, rolling backwards and forwards, recoiling into each scoring strike as I tried to keep myself safe when I heard their loud, alarmed voices.

"Leave her alone!" they had shouted.

"Come," they had called to me. "We'll pull you over the wall."

But I couldn't get to them. I was trapped in the revolutions of his charge. I was caught up in his feet. I couldn't get away as he kicked me.

He kicked me.

It is a terrible thing to be kicked.

It is dehumanising and debasing.

I was kicked like a piece of dead meat.

I was a nothing.

But I will quieten my thoughts. I don't want to think about being kicked; instead I will listen as my neighbour testifies how he and his son rushed to my property to break the door down in their attempt to get me out. He will state the accused smelt of alcohol, that he was terribly abusive as he swore at my neighbour and his son.

The defence advocate will then take the stand to cross-examine him and will vehemently deny that the accused has ever seen him.

When Sandra wraps up her matter tomorrow I will feel lighter.

I will leave the court and go home to my child, less burdened knowing that we are closer to the end.

But first there is today.

The magistrate enters and, as his eyes shift over the courtroom, he takes his place.

He reminds me that I'm still under oath.

The defence advocate stands; he takes his position and looks ahead, always past me, as though I am not just a few metres from his side.

He picks up where we left off three months earlier. The phone records. There are fifty-eight phone calls to be analysed, considered, discussed, questioned and re-questioned, harassed about, pressed on and pestered over.

It takes hours.

I respond, contend, explain, espouse and defend evenly through all these hours. I have no other choice.

I listen carefully as he intones nasally. I know I cannot let my guard down. I need to listen and watch all the time.

And that is when I see it.

The defence attorney, who is sitting at the table as the advocate harangues me, leans forward, his black jacket scrunching untidily around his shoulders. I am sure it is an extremely expensive jacket because his services come at a prohibitive premium, but it looks cheap, crumpled and dangling sloppily over his shoulders. It looks as though he has taken it from the floor and dragged it over him in a rush. He is unkempt and his hair is again slicked back into a ponytail, although it looks better than when it hangs loose. He presses on his elbows, resting his arms on the table as though he wants to flatten out my voice. His fleshy lips fold into a grimace over his big teeth. Then he looks to the magistrate.

He lifts his eyebrows and rolls his black eyes. He reels them upward as though nothing could be duller or less interesting, more boring, than my answers and my public destruction.

I throw my eyes to the magistrate.

I am quick enough.

I see it.

I see the magistrate nod. His matte-brown head bobs up and down in the very briefest of acknowledgements. It is a fleeting flash but I have seen it. I want to stop the case. I want to stand up and protest. I want to shout them down and call them out for what they have just done.

But I can't.

I am in the magistrate's domain.

I cannot object.

I look from one to the other disbelievingly.

I look around and realise that no one else has seen it. No one else is able to see it. It is only me who has this vantage point.

I look from the magistrate to the defence attorney, to the defence advocate and then to the accused. They are joined in their maleness. They are on that side of the divide. All of them.

This side of the courtroom are Sandra and me, and to my left sit my mother, Sheryl, Karen, Estie, Sue, Robyn and Katherine.

It is Them against Us.

It is patriarchy at its finest and I am defenceless against it.

I have no one to turn to.

I draw myself in.

I am shivering. It is chilly outside, but in here I am even colder. I have not dressed warmly. I am wearing a grey dress with a tailored jacket. It is another of my newsreader suits, but it is too light, the fabric too delicate to keep me warm. I lift my head to where the sunlight sneaks in. The window is high above me. It is small, the glass frosted. The sky hangs low, the sun weak as it filters through into a faded cone. I see the dust particles bumping around in the feeble light.

There is a bird perched on the sill outside, a grey pigeon distorted behind the glass. It beats its wings. It flaps around and ruffles its tail. I think it is going to take flight but it doesn't. It settles down as though it has resigned itself to its circumstances. It is a bird on a ledge.

And further away, beyond the confines of the courtroom, I hear the steady drip of water. It is the outlet pipe of an air conditioner. On the other side of the courtyard. I listen as each drop falls to the concrete, each one alone in its loss.

Twenty-five

My mother is with me. She has once again arrived in Johannesburg far earlier than is necessary and has been waiting for a while by the time I step out of the Radio Park reception. I have no understanding of what lies beneath her surface but it is all it has become, as though the past was her burden alone, as if my court case is an isolated event, that it is not preceded by a lifetime of violence. So we will not talk of anything meaningful as we forsake the leafiness of Auckland Park for the gridlock that is Empire Road. I know not to discuss or question, to interfere, because she will concede nothing. She suppresses and denies. It is her way.

We quieten as we cross the Braamfontein bridge, suspended ever so briefly above the mesh of railway lines and sidings that interlace the steel terrain below, before we enter the heart of the city centre. Simmonds Street is already bustling with pavement entrepreneurs hurriedly hustling for business as they rearrange their stalls in the hope of a new day and new season. Spring has sprung, and has brought with it an avowal of renewal.

In the far distance the mine dumps glow with the promise of prosperity.

The morning is breathless with the expectation of new beginnings.

But I am not a part of this reawakening.

As I negotiate the traffic, I am unable to let go of the past and embrace the new. Today I do not feel optimistic. I do not have a favourable view of my immediate future.

I left the last court session three months earlier, buoyed with the finality of the prosecution having rested its case. It was an enormous relief to no longer be sitting alone, fending off the defence team. I had arrived home to hold my son close and, as I cradled his head to my chest, I had assured him.

"It'll soon be over. I promise."

But one month later Sheryl received a letter from the defence notifying her that they were withdrawing and would no longer be representing the accused. There is no further explanation.

So as I turn into Fox Street I am fraught with anxiety.

The court case cannot continue if he has no representation – and what if we have to start all over, from the beginning? It is a harrowing and crippling thought.

Then there are the rumours that he is no longer around, that he may have left the country – but I have no evidence of that being true.

My mother and I once again meet with Sheryl on the steps of the courthouse. We make our way to the courtrooms below and join my familiar court supporters. We nest together like twittering fledglings and warble and trill at the possibility that the accused might have flown the coop. It is a defeating possibility. But it is not only us; Sandra is also aware of the defence team withdrawing and she hasn't received any notification of new counsel being appointed either.

I have yet to see her and I suspect she might be conferring with the magistrate.

We wait.

It is 09:20.

It is not long after that there is a rush of activity. A furious flurry. Sandra appears with the magistrate close behind. Their capes are billowing, their sleeves flapping in the air like the wings of black birds. Sandra stalks toward the court, toward me. She is like one of two ravens bringing ill omen between the shadows of ghosts, interceding between life and death, ominous and portentous. If they are raven, then they are collectively known as an 'unkindness' or a 'conspiracy'. And it looks as though they are. An unkind conspiracy, conspiring to close in on me.

Sandra shakes her head as she nears us. Her forehead is furrowed in frustration and her message is clear.

He is not here.

The magistrate takes his position behind his bench and then confirms that the accused is not present and the court case is postponed. There is no hint of outrage or disbelief to his announcement. He dismisses the court and exits. He leaves no vacuity behind. He has neither a rousing presence nor a provocative absence. He is simply no longer in the room.

My mother returns to Brits and I go home.

Once I am alone I pick up the phone and contact the police station. I need to speak to my investigating officer. I want to know what I can expect and her next course of action.

"Hello, officer," I say, my voice soft and defeated. "It's me, Tracy Going. I'm just phoning to find out what happens next."

The response from Investigating Officer No. 3 is a screeching squall that pitches right through me.

"I dunno!" she shouts. "I didn't ask him to run away!"

I am silent.

She is a police officer, and my presiding investigator. I am flabbergasted.

"What do you mean?" I ask.

"What do you want me to do?" she snaps. "It's not my fault he ran away."

"Thank you," I say.

I put the phone down.

It is the only conversation I ever have with her.

○

The accused's bail is withdrawn and a warrant of arrest is issued, but it changes nothing for me as I am left floundering.

The rumours are rife. It is whispered that he's in East Africa, hiding out somewhere between Dar es Salaam and Zanzibar. I know his brother has development projects on the go in the region so it makes sense that he would take flight there, but still I am astonished. I am shaken to my inner, crumbling core. It is unbelievable that he has absconded. It is not only preposterous – it is absolutely and unequivocally shameful.

I am bewildered and I am angry, and I am determined not to let him get away.

I contact the office of the Police Commissioner George Fivaz and ask to speak to him personally. I am put onto one of the national deputy commissioners instead, and I meet with him for coffee. I want the accused's name entered into the database of Interpol. I want his name engraved on the list of fugitives. I insist.

The deputy police commissioner assures me that a man fleeing the law can only run so hard, so far and so fast.

It would take one year to catch him.

I would wait.

But waiting is an adjournment. It is an obstruction between now and one day, whenever. It is the infancy of uncertainty, depression and isolation. And the months ahead bleed into each other as I try to maintain control over my life and contain my despair while I wait.

I am still co-anchoring the radio breakfast show and presenting my TV show, *Lebone – Women on the Move*. I rise in the morning, do what is necessary and collapse onto my bed in between, as I slowly lose all my ability to face the light.

I joined Summit TV as an evening *Business News* anchor a few months before and am now broadcasting from there two nights a week. I am extremely grateful to be appointed to the team of heavyweight presenters when so many are hesitant of being tainted by me and my court case.

But in between I put living and dreaming aside.

I am no longer producing a weekly insert for the magazine programme *Private & Confidential*, but producer Pieter hasn't discarded me. Soon after the accused flees, Pieter puts together a programme on intercultural healing. He wants me to consult a sangoma for one of the inserts, and I am willing. I am searching for guidance and answers and am content to surrender myself to the unknown.

It is the sage words of the sangoma that enable me to process in advance, and then help me to accept, that I am voiceless and that, despite all my best efforts, I cannot alter the outcome. My testimony in court, and my exhausting and debilitating fight for justice, will come to almost naught. It is inevitable. I am defenceless against the money, the power, the patriarchy, all the lies and deception. I am impotent against the biased reasoning of a court where there is no insight or understanding or compassion to even begin to comprehend the complexity of power and control an abuser exercises over a victim.

Selby, the sangoma, operates from a small cottage in a back garden of a home in Melville. It is a dark room and the air hangs dense with the rich, sweet smell of smouldering *impepho*, the perfumed plant of the past. It is a sacred herb, with a flower that never withers and the divine purpose of bringing clarity to healers and diviners. Selby, with his open, engaging face and generous, enveloping embrace, is a bone diviner.

He is already burning *impepho* and calling on the spirits to bring their presence and their 'remembering' when I enter the cottage. Graciously, he sits me down and explains that he'd be connecting with his ancestors and other departed souls to bring me the messages I most need to hear. I am entranced.

We then kneel opposite each other on the carpet before crossing our legs beneath us and settling into the reading.

He unties his soft, thin, black cloth bag and spreads it out between us. He removes its precious contents – the bones, stones, coins and other valued bits – and holds them delicately in his hands before he closes his eyes, to keel and to clap as he invokes the ancestors.

There is a melodic chant as he ventures into the past. Then, quickly, he opens his hands and flings the contents from his palm. He tosses them away, casting them out onto the flat black cloth.

"You are in danger," he says cautiously. "You must protect your walls. There is someone looking in."

He opens his eyes, his stare vacant, as though his mind is not in this realm.

I look back, my eyes stretched wide.

"You must be careful," he says, his voice low and ominous.

"Yes," I answer softly.

Sitting directly across from him, I wonder what he has really seen. Is he speaking to ancestral spirits from the grave, is he really receiving this message through the dry bones of the dead, or is it simply me carrying the stink of fear like decaying flesh falling from bones?

He speaks of many other things before he collects all his pieces together, wraps them back into the black cloth and puts the bundle aside. Then he passes me a length of rope. It is an ordinary rope made of white fibre with edges unravelling from years of gentle handling. He instructs me to tie a knot. He takes the knotted rope from my hands, holds it lightly, tumbles it around a little and then throws it out.

It lies before me like a rope with a knot.

"There is a matter," he says. "It is a legal matter."

"Yes," I say, breathless.

He is quiet as he unties the knot, freeing it of its tension. He looks at me knowingly.

"You will win," he breathes. "But not in the way you want."

Twenty-six

"Bruce, you're hurting me!"

It is my mother screaming.

I can hear her agony through the haze of my sleep, through the closed door of my bedroom. It is the first time I've heard her in such pain and, as I leap from my bed and bolt across the room, I know instantly that this time it is different. I grab at the door, yank it open and launch myself down the passage, closer to her blood-curling screams.

I can hear my father's heavy grunts.

I know he has her in the bathroom.

Then suddenly I am screaming too.

"No, Dad, you're hurting her," I shout, my sobs and screams mingling as one.

"Please let her go," I beg. "Please, Dad, please!"

I am standing in the doorway, framed in the fluorescent light of the bathroom as it spills into the darkness of the passage. My father is holding my mother by her mouth, his hand holding her lower jaw. He has her bottom lip in his grip, twisting it viciously, holding it as though in a vice as he smashes her head repeatedly into the corner of the bath, on the sharp edge where the green tiles meet.

I get there just in time to see him leaning over her, smacking her head down hard, before tightening his hold and hauling her up toward him again.

"No, Dad. Let her go," I cry.

He straightens, and as he glowers at me in his alcoholic rage, he loses his grip.

My mother is a broken bundle on the tiles, her nightie torn from her shoulders.

"Be careful," she mumbles. "He's going to hurt you."

Her words are bloodied and indistinct as she mumbles her warning, gesturing weakly.

"Don't worry, Mom," I assure her, wrenching myself out of his reach as he lurches after me. "He's too drunk to catch me."

Then I run.

I run as fast as I can, him stumbling behind me, falling forward, groaning with each grab, his stale beer breath warm on my neck, my back. It is only in the dining room that I manage to gain enough distance between us that I can unlatch a window and leap out into the night.

But I have nowhere to go. Just the dark gloom of late night.

The water tank towers above me but offers no refuge, nowhere to hide. I don't want to run off into the black veld.

Then I hear him shouting, calling my name.

"Tracy!"

He is around the other side of the house. I know that any minute now he's going to come careening around the corner, staggering into his charge, and he'll find me easily, my pale, fleecy pyjamas beckoning like a beacon, a guiding light in the dark.

"Tracy!" I hear. "I'm going to find you!"

My father is going to hurt me.

◯

Another flashback. Always the same intense, uninvited memory crashing through my mind, twisting and turning before me, tormenting me as I try to escape. It is a relentless recollection from the past; the night I ran and hid from my father.

I was eleven years old. It was the middle of the night and I had no idea where to run to. I remember hiding close to the stone wall, outside my mother's sewing room. I had no slippers on my feet. I could hear my father's voice in the distance. He was shouting out my name. It sounded slurred and strangled, as though he already had his hands around my neck. I knew I needed to get away. I knew I needed to find somewhere to hide – and then I remembered that the pool was standing empty for the winter. It was my only refuge, the white, hollow haven to the side of the house ... between him and me. That meant I needed to move in his direction, toward him, to get away. I clutched at the uneven edges of the stone to guide myself along the wall in the dark. I crouched down low, listening for his shouts to determine exactly where he was, and then I crept across the garden and slid silently into the pool. I curled into a ball, pulled my pyjama top over my head and buried myself tight against the steps, camouflaging myself against the whiteness and the cold.

Later, I heard him leave, heard the key in the ignition of his car and the spray of pebbles and sand as he took off, perhaps he thought I had run away. Once he had been gone long enough, I found the courage to tiptoe back into the house. I crawled under my bed, making certain that none of me was sticking out. And then I waited for the morning.

It is fleeting flashes of this memory that so disturb me, always coming back, refusing to leave, shadowing me in and out of my consciousness with no regard for time or place.

It comes in the glint of glass, a pot falling, a stranger's glance.

It is involuntary and relentless and soon the darkness has so invaded my being that I completely yield to it in my search for oblivion. For nine months I sleep and I sleep and I eat; boxes and boxes of biscuits offering me comfort in my pain. I lift myself to work, then I come home and I cry and I sleep and I eat. It is all I am able to do.

In December, I force myself from my slumber and haul myself out of bed to attend the official opening of the 16 Days of Activism campaign. It is the year this international awareness campaign opposing violence against women and children is introduced in

South Africa. The event is a spectacular affair, with a thousand guests, among them leading business people and their spouses, socialites, politicians and parliamentarians.

I am the professional Master of Ceremonies for the night. I am a woman who has been abused – it is a fitting profile. I am wearing a ballgown that fans spectacularly around me. On the outside I'm elegant and glamorous, but inside I am vulnerable, frail with fatigue, and hopelessly overwhelmed by my own circumstances. I am completely ill equipped to cope with the evening.

It is my role to guide everyone through a tribute paid to women who'd lost their lives to violence. It has been rehearsed that as I raise my hand in honour to those murdered at the hands of their abusers, the lights to the decorated venue would be switched off and the room would be thrown into a dramatic, crushing darkness. It is then that every single person, each one having received a candle as they entered, would light it in remembrance. At every table one match would be struck, and then the candle would go from person to person, symbolically passing the flame, until the room is awash with 1000 candles flickering flimsily before being silently snuffed out.

As arcs of fluttering white and gold sweep across the room and delicately infuse the darkness, I break. I disintegrate, right there before everyone. I heave and gasp my anguish as I fall apart, and then flee the room.

I am inconsolable. It is only an hour later that I am able to collect myself enough to take to the stage, and make a gasping, mortifying apology, before excusing myself and escaping home, back to my bed.

I should never have been there.

It had all been too much.

Then, another day, I wake to find my son lying on the floor. It is late afternoon and I have spent the entire day in my bed. Sleeping. I am disoriented when I'm woken by his screams. He is beneath my wrought-iron bed, kicking his short legs and flailing his small arms as he cries.

"You're always sleeping," he shouts, his words muffled between his tears.

"I'm sorry," I stutter.

And I am. I am sorry. But I am incapable of giving more than a mumbled apology, unable to lift myself from the pillow. All I want is to disappear, to retreat into obscurity, to surrender myself to my dependable companion: darkness.

○

It is months later that I am passing through my hallway. The front door is locked and latched as it always is. The hallway is dim and gloomy in the dusk, the last red and orange of the day filtering through the ribbed, glass panels when I briefly catch my reflection in the mirror over the server, the same server that supposedly held a serrated knife so long ago. I am not surprised by what I see. It is the shapeless form of the new me. I am thirteen kilogrammes heavier, my hair hanging limp, my skin inflamed. I am a mess. I realise then how I've allowed him and his violence to define me.

I have abandoned myself.

For so long I have struggled to keep myself, my life and my son's life together after he destroyed it, but it is when he fled that I lost my inner bearing. As I look at that shadowed self in the mirror I know I can never reclaim the person I had been before, that I have forever been altered, but I know too that there is no other way to work through the pain, the hurt and the confusion than to collect together the fragments of my beaten, broken self and somehow meld it all together again.

It is time.

I am more than a battered woman.

I lean forward to confirm that the bruises are gone, and they are; they are long gone and my eyes are crystal clear, but it is then – as so often happens when I look in a mirror – that I am instantly reminded of my father.

I have my father's dark, blue eyes.

It's all I have of him really.

My father left Brits and our life with his briefcase in one hand and his ornate mantelpiece clock in the other. At the age of forty-two they were his only meaningful possessions. By fifty-two he was dead, and those two items were long gone. At some point over the intervening years they had been bartered in his desperation for just one more bottle. It had been my childhood request that one day he bequeath the clock to me. I loved its carved wood façade, the slow and steady rhythm of its beat, the tinkle of its chime. It had belonged to my great-grandparents. But now it is gone, and instead, after my father's death, I was given a photo of him as a child, a copy of his ID and a small, black Bible.

I had placed them in a box in an unused cupboard in my study, forgotten.

I recently took them out.

The photo is still between the glass and its collapsing frame. The copy of his ID has damped over time and the folded page is joined as one where the running ink has fused it together. My father's face is still visible, however, and so too is the madness in his eyes. I toss it out and then quickly retrieve it from the bin, thinking perchance another day.

It's only the Bible I really want to keep safe. It is a small, beautifully illustrated, very, very old book. The spine has disintegrated and the pages are flaking apart. It is the first time I ever open it, and find the palest inscription on the inside cover. It is addressed, in the finest point of blue ink, to my grandparents: *Philip and May, with regards and best wishes for the future, from Arthur Lee 1939*. I have no idea who Arthur Lee is and I can only conclude that it had been a thoughtful wedding present to my late grandparents.

As I page through it now I find two loose, dulled blue papers. They are the original birth certificates of my twin brother and sister. They take my breath away as I unfurl and read them.

They were issued, and written by hand, one week after their birth, on 12 May 1969. My sister was born at 1:30 am and my brother, David Bruce Going, listed as Twin No. II, at 2:00 am. The birth certificates are boldly inscribed in black fountain-pen ink and as I hold them in my hands I realise that they offer no indication of what lies ahead. It tells me nothing of the life my sister will live, and gives no hint of my brother's death. All it tells me is that my father has kept these papers safe for many years. In the end, they were his most valuable possession.

I carefully fold them back along their crease lines and return them to where I found them, between the delicate pages of Leviticus. And then, as I close the Bible, with its loose black faux-leather cover, I see a name. It is written in very feint, faded blue and I have to look closely to decipher the small writing. It reads, *Margaret*. My father's sister. I realise that, after all these years of keeping it safe, the Bible is not my father's after all. It belongs to his sister.

So all I really have is that photograph. A garish picture of him as a young boy with rosy cheeks. It is an image that has been enhanced in a studio. It bears little resemblance to the child he must have been.

And now he is gone. I will never receive an apology or an explanation, and I simply have to accept the violence he has bestowed on me. But I will always be his eldest, "my girl". As his daughter, I can only hope that he wanted his life to be different, and that he had wanted more. And also as his daughter I can only hope, I need to believe, that he would have wanted more for me, for my life to be different.

But being a father's daughter tells me I belong. It tells me I have a place in this world, that I am worthy.

Twenty-seven

"We've found him," says the deputy commissioner heartily, triumph in his voice.

"No!" I shout, clutching my phone to my ear. "Where?"

"Zimbabwe. He's been arrested."

It is unbelievable. It seems he'd been arrested on unrelated assault and drug charges. He had apparently been detained for about two weeks in prison before anyone realised he was a fugitive from South Africa and wanted by Interpol. He was escorted back to Johannesburg and detained at the Parkview police station for a few days before appearing before the magistrate.

I have no need to attend court. I have no interest in seeing him arrive shackled at the courtroom. I do not hanker after his humiliation; I want only accountability and justice, so Sheryl attends his court appearance on my behalf.

"You're not going to believe it," she announces soon after.

"What?" I ask over the phone.

"He's out."

"What do you mean *he's out*?" I am astounded.

"The magistrate said, 'I believe this man deserves another chance.'"

"*Another chance?*"

I am outraged but not surprised. I am not in the least bit taken aback that the magistrate thinks this man deserves another chance.

I read in a newspaper the next day that even the accused's new attorney appeared stunned by the outcome of the application for bail. I, however, am not. I am not amazed at all.

I then read in *The Citizen* that "the proceedings were attended by Ms Going". But they weren't. I hadn't attended. It is yet another inaccurate report by the paper's court reporter. The reporter goes on to explain that the accused has been given bail and that "Ms Going appeared less than pleased at this prospect".

How could I have appeared less than pleased when I wasn't even there, I fume.

I had long since given up taking umbrage at some of the media reports that left me feeling sullied, but this particular court reporter and her reporting is without doubt the most offensive. She titles her stories disrespectfully, headlining with: 'Tale of lovers' fury retold.'

And then she commences the piece with: "Further evidence of the soured relationship between radio and TV personality Ms Tracy Going, and beverage company owner XXX, with volatile scenes worthy of the best soap operas, unfolded yesterday ..."

I am incensed, insulted. I feel my throat closing up. This is not a soap opera – it's my life, and her acerbic words dirty me more. I'm further offended and degraded when she writes of "the airing of dirty laundry".

The latest report detailing the accused being released on bail is titled 'Guilty plea now to attacking TV girl'. I am insulted – I'm not a *girl*. I'm a hard-working, successful woman, a responsible, caring mother, and I am fighting to reclaim myself.

I am aggrieved when she presents the defence's allegations as 'fact' and offsets them with my denial. My observation is strengthened by the headline: 'Presenter "seeking financial gain"'. It immediately creates the impression that I'm doing it all for the money, and anything beyond that is thus irrelevant. Even if I repudiate it, undoubtedly the image in the reader's mind remains that I am seeking to gain financially from this entire ordeal.

As a journalist and as a woman, she has a moral and ethical

obligation to respect my pain as the victim. I am being stripped bare and exposed in the courtroom and her slanted hostility re-victimises me and further rubs my nakedness in shame. I consider her reporting to be reckless, but her enmity had already been apparent in the courtroom.

I would watch her out in the courtyard with the accused, hear her throaty smoker's laugh as she threw back her head at his fascinating, funny words. I would see the ritual of the knowing look, the colluding smile, before she tipped her bottle-blonde head and he flicked the lighter to her thin cigarette. I would feel the chill down my back as they stood close, inhaling deeply together, before breathing out as one.

She is an ageing court reporter, her face heavily lined beneath a yellowed fringe and cheeks creased with bitterness, perhaps with life in general. It seems her resentment and disappointment bleed through her words, but her writing is so skewered and so inaccurate and I am so humiliated that I cannot let it go. I feel obliged to address it, a responsibility to not allow this to happen – to me, to anyone.

Charlene is equally outraged and through her I am given the opportunity to voice my objection. She contacts the editor of *The Citizen* newspaper and demands some form of apology or retraction. Then she further commands the opportunity to address the insensitivity of the judiciary overall, and the media in particular.

She writes a lengthy article on how the media, when their reporting is irresponsible and reckless, put women at risk and how the bias of the 'observer' means that there is no safe haven for women in danger. She questions the role of the media when they claim to "report in the interests of society" and yet they "blithely criticise". She asks the media to consider what their role has been in reducing the incredible trauma of survivors of violent crime and in combating criminality. She then poses the question: "Is the media lazy, or does it fit in with the general insensitivity we ascribe to the judiciary – of not realising that violent crime does not happen on a particular day, at a particular time. For survivors it has traumatic long-term effects that last months or years."

I am so grateful to have Charlene at my side, and I will be alongside her through her rape trial that had already got underway.

I hadn't known her before. I was familiar with who she was, given her high profile as a journalist, but I only got to know her after I started following her harrowing rape case in the media. It was a photograph emblazoned across the front page of a newspaper, of her walking out of court, that had touched me so. I had been drawn to her instantly. It was the pain in her eyes. Perhaps I saw myself in her wretchedness. I sent an enormous bouquet of flowers. I thought she deserved some beauty and gentleness. She had phoned to thank me and we had connected.

It was only a year later – after me sitting on a long, wooden bench in court, this time in support of her – that I had come home to Wilhemina's chilling announcement. She knew I'd gone to court and she'd listened to the news on the radio.

"You know that man, the one who raped your friend, you met him."

Her words choked me.

"What do you mean, I met him?" I asked incredulously.

She had then gone on to remind me of one languid Saturday afternoon when I had been on my veranda reading and she had walked past me in the garden with her friend and her friend's boyfriend. I remembered the introduction immediately. It had been mid-afternoon. They were walking ahead of Wilhemina, laughing and talking loudly, holding hands, when she had called them back to introduce them to me. They had stopped, greeted me effusively and then left.

He was Charlene's rapist. The one who'd smiled so jauntily.

I was nauseated. I felt blemished. I felt as though somehow I'd invited this unimaginable, unbearable, abhorrent violation into her life even though I hadn't known her then.

But perhaps Charlene's and my meeting had not been by chance. There have been many times that I thought it was intended, like some inescapable destiny, predetermined, that we would be there for each other, to walk alongside each other as we took action against our personal defilements and the injustice that followed.

And her outrage and her action now, against the injustice of the reporter's pointed pen, offered a ripple of hope and vindication.

Ironically, it is an article by the same court reporter – if her reporting is to be believed – that informs me of the latest developments: the accused, as part of his new bail conditions, is to reside with his brother just a few kilometres away from where I am living.

According to her report, it seems his brother has glibly and seemingly generously undertaken in court to negotiate and make good on 'reasonable' claims from me, as part of the motivation for the accused being released on bail. This is the same brother who, along with the accused, and according to the accused, allegedly sued their mother for their inheritance so many years before. I would never receive any form of 'reasonable' restitution. I would receive nothing. My civil trial would come to an end only after the criminal trial, after his guilty conviction, and I would be awarded a 'reasonable' compensation by the court, but that was it. No attempt would ever be made by the accused to remunerate this 'reasonable compensation' even after a court ruling. And there appears to be nothing in the judicial system that enforces this ruling either. He would never pay.

He would never be made to pay.

In fact, the accused finds no need to even appear in court for the civil trial. It will be his attorney alone on that day. And after the trial, when Sheryl contacts his attorney to finalise the court outcome, he will inform her that he no longer represents the accused and is therefore unable to forward our claim. To me his actions, his response, are dishonourable and shameful.

But by then I have no more fight in me.

For now, however, I am still able to gather myself together and pursue the trial to its weak end.

The accused brings in a new attorney, who changes the plea to guilty. He changes his argument and his new defence is that he has a drug problem. He denies that he had run from justice and, instead, claims that he ran from drugs, to get away from the drug scene. I read in the newspapers that when he is arrested in Zimbabwe, a few weeks earlier, there are unspecified drug charges.

But, he tells the court, he is clean of drugs and has been since his 'fortunate escape' a year earlier.

It is Friday, 17 September 1999, when he comes before the magistrate to be given bail again and is released with the comfort that he "deserves another chance". His bail had initially been revoked and a warrant of arrest issued for him on 17 September 1998. It had taken one year, to the day, to reapprehend him and bring him back to court.

The magistrate sets the next court appearance for 25 October 1999. He battered my life apart on 25 October 1997.

It is exactly two years to the day.

Twenty-eight

Today he is testifying.
Today he will take the oath and present his defence.
I have spent much time speculating as to whether the defence attorney will allow his client to take the stand or not. I am part of the prosecution, which means I have no idea in advance as to who will eventually be called to attest. It will be a surprise to us all. But I know that if I was a defence attorney and he my client, I would prefer that he keep quiet. I would find his arrogance disconcerting. I would find his over-confidence, that he can 'beat' the system, alarming because that makes him unpredictable. And I can't think of much worse for a defence attorney than a client who is unmanageable. But I know the accused, and I know he will want to testify – in fact, I believe he will insist on testifying.
I walk into the courtroom, and glance over at the new defence attorney. I have never seen him before. He has brown hair and appears a little thickened around the middle. He tips his head toward me in greeting. I am taken by surprise. This is the first time I have ever been acknowledged by any member of the defence team. It is completely disarming. Perhaps it is a strategy all defence attorneys should use in the courtroom, because from then on I commiserate with him. I pity him having to represent such a despicable man. But everyone is entitled to a defence, I know that much.

I imagine it can't have been easy to find a new defence attorney half way through a trial, after you've skipped the country and been arrested for another violation. I suspect the new attorney must have put certain conditions in place, which is why the accused is now pleading guilty. It is possibly a strategy to minimise the damages of what can only be considered to be a losing matter by many – either that, or the attorney thinks there's a possibility of a sympathetic magistrate. That would be enormously helpful in defending a man who's beaten up a woman and run from justice.

Once the court is in session, the defence calls his client to the box. The accused stands directly opposite Sandra and me, a few metres away. He is close, close enough for me to see the expression in his brown eyes.

His navy-blue jacket hangs from his shoulders, shapeless, worn and thin, but perhaps it is just me who is tired of seeing it. He is wearing a blue shirt today, but it is the same green-and-red striped tie, the same chinos and the same brown suede shoes.

It strains my eyes to look at him.

He is a terrible witness. He shifts from one foot to another, moving constantly. He has a sheaf of paper in front of him and he keeps knocking the pages off the stand. He bends down a few times to pick up the scattered leaves. He tells how I lunged at him with a knife and how he put up his arm to defend himself. He waves his arms about as he explains. He lifts his arm and brings it over his face to demonstrate how he protected himself against me. He ducks. He raises his leg, his knee is up high; he extends his lower leg, and stretches it forward to indicate how I managed to get beneath him and under his foot to slash it with a knife. As he kicks, he knocks over his papers again. He leans down to pick them up, and as he gathers them together his pen falls from his pocket. It rolls. It keeps rolling. It rolls out the witness box, away from him. He watches it. He stretches, reaches out for it, before resigning himself to the loss. He straightens and tells how his feet were bare. He continues with his testimony. Slowly he becomes more grandiose in the details and braver in the telling. He talks of how I threw vases at him. It is the first I hear of vases and ornaments being thrown.

I turn to look at his attorney; I suspect he would like to cut his client short.

He is nodding curtly. He has no expression on his face; he's keeping it tight and still. It is a similar expression to the one I use when I try to discourage a guest from talking too much during an interview when time is limited. I nod quickly in rapid succession, a very subtle gesture, to silently encourage an end to a point that is being made. It is a skill I am learning on my new TV show, presenting the national breakfast show, *Morning Live*.

So, when I see the defence attorney curtly nodding his head, I know he is discouraging his client from rambling on, suggesting he wrap it up, but the accused is completely oblivious. He is talking very long and very loudly.

I whisper again to Sandra that he's lying.

"Don't worry," she says, squeezing my arm.

But I do.

The magistrate is rapt as he listens to the accused. He appears very interested.

The accused testifies that he is a reformed man. He states that he is going for therapy and drug counselling. He blames the past on his drug abuse.

I am exhausted just watching him.

Then it is Sandra's turn to put her questions to him. I watch her as she pushes her chair out, stands and pulls her black gown forward, away from her shoulders, before pulling it closed in the front. It is her unwittingly cloaking herself in prosecutorial rightness, but I know it isn't enough.

The transformation in the accused is instant. He lifts his chin defiantly. He clasps his hands behind his back and he thrusts his hips out forward. His lips are twisted thin as he looks down at her. He cuts her words short as he interrupts, sneering and snorting his replies.

"Why did you previously deny taking drugs and now, after all this time, that is your defence?"

He blames his previous attorney and advocate. He states baldly that they advised him that his drug problem was irrelevant. It was their fault entirely.

There is a stir in the courtroom as everyone sniggers disbelievingly.

The magistrate looks around accusingly and frowns at my mother, my friends and the journalists leaning forward on the benches.

The accused then goes on to explain the limitation of his past drug habit.

"The problem with drugs is that it lowers your standards," he says.

He is unable to contain himself, he glances over at me and smirks. It is a slash across his face. I remain impassive. I want my face unreadable. I don't want him to know that I still flinch at his brutality.

"She's not my sort," he says, sneering.

There is no end to his insults and rudeness.

"If I wanted a wife I'd buy a wife."

I am relieved when it is all over.

He has been on the stand for three hours. I can't help but be bitter at the injustice that I, the victim, had been on the stand for three long, gruelling, torturous days and he, the accused, is only there for three hours.

It is unfair and unjust.

The magistrate adjourns the court for lunch.

Thereafter the defence attorney will call the expert witnesses. The role of the defence has mostly been to cast aspersions on my testimony, to call me a liar and a cheat, but now, as the matter reaches its heady conclusion, the role of the defence is to bring in the independent expert, and to provide paid testimony that might make us question who the real victim is.

It is here that I step back as though I am in a movie. To me it is like a film script unravelling before my eyes:

"Is the real victim not the man who lifted his elbow in defence? Is it not the man who was re-arrested, shackled and humiliated when he was escorted back into the country? Does this man not deserve our empathy at worst and our support at best? Does he not deserve an opportunity to put the past behind him and honour his future?"

It all feels so unreal that I try to escape into the recesses of my mind.

But his psychologist's words quickly bring me back.

She testifies how I hit him.

She, the expert witness, tells *how I hit him*.

I grab desperately at Sandra.

"It's okay," she whispers.

But it's not. It is not okay. There is nothing fine about an expert witness presenting hearsay as fact. She then mentions that the accused has, admittedly, also told her of an incident where he had been violent with his ex-girlfriend. It is uttered so quickly it is as though it has never been said.

Then it is the turn of the addiction counsellor.

As her name is called out and she steps into the booth to swear her allegiance to the truth, I recognise her. I know her from a time when I needed to believe in grown-ups.

As her heels break the silence of the cold floor and she moves closer to the box to share her knowledge and her expertise, I realise that she looks smaller. Although she is at least six feet tall, she's not quite as imposing as I remember. I watch as she nods at the magistrate and then she glances around the courtroom, confident in her knowledge.

She won't remember me from when I was fourteen years old but I will always remember her.

Today I am deeply, deeply saddened.

Today I feel as though the ground is shaking beneath me when I realise that this woman, who I have revered my entire life, who gave me insight, understanding and explanation, who gave me hope, is not on my side.

Today, she is an 'expert witness' for the defence, one whose testimony is accounted for by the hour.

Today, with authority, assurance and strength, she will tell the magistrate and everyone present that, despite his years of addiction and violence, the accused is a man deserving of his freedom. He is a man, in her opinion, who has shown remorse and can easily be rehabilitated. She is unwavering in her professional knowledge. She is an authority. She knows and she tells.

As I sit watching and listening, I remember how all those many years ago she gave me no promise that my father would ever change. In fact, she insisted that in all probability he would never be otherwise, that he'd never be anyone else besides the person he already was. Instead, she encouraged me to accept what was, to not focus on what would doubtless never be, to rather become the person I foresaw and live the life I dreamt of living.

But today she testifies differently. Today, in her brevity, she assures us that the accused is a changed man.

I cannot believe her.

Twenty-nine

It is Tuesday, 8 February 2000, and today I wear black. A black jacket, black trousers, black camisole and black high-heel shoes. It is not a colour recommended for broadcasting. I seldom wear it on camera because it absorbs the light and it reflects as dull and lifeless.

I draw my curtain aside to peer out at the developing day. It is 04:00. Pre-dawn, but already it is overcast, cloudy outside. The sky is dark and dense.

At the studio I present the breakfast show. Afterwards I meet my mother in the parking lot and we make our way through town to the magistrate's court where I am to take my seat beside Sandra for the very last time. My friends Karen, Estie, Sue, Robyn, Katherine and Charlene are inside the courtroom waiting when my mother, Sheryl and I arrive. The remaining court benches are packed with radio and print journalists.

It is 09:00 when the magistrate enters.

Today we will hear him speak.

As he straightens his black gown and begins with his judgment I am still a little hopeful that I have underestimated and misread the outcome. I listen intently as he speaks.

"I find this matter to be an isolated incident through provocation ..."

An isolated incident.

I feel the colour draining from my face.

I hear the collective gasp of incredulousness around me. It is not only me who cannot believe he has just said those words.

An isolated incident through provocation, even after the accused's own psychologist testified, albeit fleetingly, in this courtroom that the accused had admitted to striking out at his previous girlfriend ...

The magistrate talks of passion. He accuses me of exaggerating the details of when I was beaten up and says, given my size, my slightness, it would have been impossible for me to survive the incident I described.

I am horrified.

He accuses me of speaking to all and sundry in the media. He says I manipulated the media and used it to my advantage. As his words echo around the court, I think of how I tried to stop the photographs from being published. I think of how destructive some of those media reports were.

I think of how, in all those years, I was only ever quoted twice: once in an article in *Fair Lady* and then again in another magazine feature. Both articles were published long after he'd skipped the country. I had talked only of my fear, my frustration and my disappointment. Because the matter was *sub judice*, I made sure that the content of each piece was based on my testimony. I was determined that nothing should jeopardise the trial.

The magistrate concludes that my "revenge has been sweet" and, he says, reminds him of the old adage, "Hell hath no fury like a woman scorned".

I listen to him no more. It is over.

I look at my mother and she is crying silently.

It is a mother's pain.

When he finally finishes and leaves the courtroom, I stand quietly. I hug Sandra. I thank her for all her hard work and commitment, all those mornings she was in her office, the dawn still damp with dew, preparing for my matter. I know her commitment and I appreciate it so. I am still standing alongside Sandra when the accused pushes past me. He slams his elbow into my arm. I look at him in horror.

He laughs in my face. It is a hard, brittle noise.

I am completely aghast.

I do nothing.

I leave the courtroom between my mother and Sheryl – there is no reason to stay – and, once I am outside in the corridor, I am approached by a radio journalist. He pushes a microphone in my direction and asks for comment. I have nothing profound to say.

"I am in shock."

After all these years, I have only four small miserable words to say about the matter.

He thanks me for my comment, but he has a viewpoint he'd like to express and announces it with almost certainty.

"Money has changed hands in this court case," he says. "It has to have!" He shakes his head, disbelievingly.

"Really, you think so?" I answer, but there is hollowness to my voice. "If it has, there's not much we can do," I continue. "But thank you."

I appreciate the sentiment, and then I turn and walk away.

It is too late. It no longer matters.

Head down, I make my way down the corridor, up the stairs and over the concourse with my mother and Sheryl trailing behind me. It was so long ago that I first followed them both through the main entrance on Fox Street, up the grand stairway, past the marble columns and statues of justice, down into the intricate passageways leading to the courtrooms. Today they are behind me as we leave through the less impressive Marshall Street exit.

I walk ahead, alone, to be greeted by throngs, women's groups and other activists. They are singing and their voices haunt the dying minutes of the gloomy morning. They are waving posters with pictures of women who have been badly injured or murdered by their intimate partners. The women are angry as they chant, they feel the sentence is too lenient. There will be more outrage by the media and other women's organisations. And so there should be, a paltry fine and a one-year sentence suspended for five years are insulting to all women.

There are also cut-out cardboard T-shirts hanging from a cord across the stairs. Each one bears a woman's name in black khoki: *Selina Ngwena (26) stabbed to death by her boyfriend* and *Brenda Mahonoe (16) killed by her boyfriend* and *Kgaogelo Swefo* and *Anna Mhlanga* ... it continues endlessly. I walk beneath the names of dead women swaying silently over me in the grey air.

I don't want to be reminded. I don't want to think about any further pain. I want to go home, home to my child. I have lived the last few years of my life consciously. I have known each day as the sun has risen and the sun has set, and now I want it over.

I am waiting at the school gate as the bell rings shrilly.

"Mommy, how did it go?" he asks breathlessly. He is smiling. He has two big front teeth. He is taller. He has grown so much over the last two-and-a-half years.

I grab him and hold him tight as he wiggles.

"It's all over, my angel. It's finished," I tell him. "Let's go home," I say, taking his school bag and his hand.

Later in the afternoon I am taken aback to receive a call from a producer at a radio station. He says he has spoken to an ex-girlfriend of the accused; she called in to say she had heard the news reports and is unimpressed by the court's findings. She wants to speak out. It is the first time I hear Cathy's name. I have known the identity of only one other ex-girlfriend, the same woman I heard the accused verbally abusing on the phone, the same woman the accused's very own psychologist admitted had been beaten up by him, but she wasn't prepared to testify.

I am so moved that finally, after all this time, there is a woman out there who is prepared to speak up for me.

The producer tells me he has suggested she contact the *Sunday Times*, so the headlines of the page that weekend reads: 'XXX beat me too – Former girlfriend tells how man who assaulted celebrity Tracy Going beat her and wrung her neck'.

In the article, Cathy tells how the accused assaulted her at least a dozen times during their brief relationship. The accused then denies ever having met her and gives his own statement: "When will this personal vendetta of hers end – with me surrendering? This whole thing is a farce – I've been demonised. Women are being beaten and emotionally butchered every day, and everyone is focusing on what was nothing more than a spat. I am personally very concerned about women's rights – people must look at the real issues, not this."

I skim over his quote quickly – I am interested only in her chilling words: "Those eight weeks were a nightmare – this great guy just changed into a monster suddenly. He threw me around often but the worst was when he wrung my neck on the bed. I thought I would die like that."

I hold the paper tight as I breathe in its cold, dried, black ink. I remember how I too thought I was going to die.

But it is over now.

He is gone.

I will never see him again. There, in that courtroom when he pushed past me and hit me in the arm with his elbow, is the very last time I see him. I was still rubbing away at my arm when I turned to see him darken the doorway and watched how those in his path gave way around him.

My final words

This has been my long journey in my search for light, understanding, and acceptance of self.

As I wrote this book, I've often asked myself: "Why? Why am I writing this?" But through all the self-doubt and the second guessing, I've also asked "Why was I given this story?" And I hope I have been right in thinking that I was given this story to tell it one day.

Writing this book, I've had to dig deep. I've had to go far back into my memory and remember. It has been long and arduous. Sometimes I've wanted to give up. But I'm so glad I didn't.

I initially started writing to offer some insight into the dynamics of the power play between an abuser and the abused. I also wanted to share what happens in the courtroom. I do not want to discourage any courageous woman from ever taking a stand, and perhaps my experience can be used in preparation for the psychological onslaught.

But, as I wrote, I realised more and more that I was actually leaving a legacy for my children. I realised that by telling them my story I could offer some understanding into why I might fall short as a person or as a mother. I want them to know that I take the blame for any damage I've unconsciously inflicted. I tell them all the time that if I've left them with any holes, I'm sorry. I will not walk away. I will not make excuses. I believe apology brings empathy and understanding, that it clears the way to the privilege of having a relationship with one's children. They've all asked whether they can read my story one day. I tell them they can read it if and when they want.

But the reason of writing for others, or for my children, paled when the more immersed I became and the more I remembered, the more I realised that, really, I wasn't actually writing for others at all – I was writing for myself.

I've had to analyse why things happened as they did. I've had to look deep inside as I examined my reactions, or non-reactions, to certain situations. I've had to ask what it says about me and whether I could have – or should have – done things differently. And through this analysing, perhaps even over-analysing, I have come to understand myself so much better. I've had to forgive myself, I've had to be kind.

Those who have held my hand through this process have often asked whether it has been cathartic. I've always thought that to be an interesting question. When I started writing, I genuinely did not think it would be purifying in any way; I'd already done all my healing, but as the words unfolded before me there have been many times when I have put my head down and sobbed, when I've stood up and walked away for the day, a week, maybe even a few weeks. But then there have been occasions when I've also thrown back my head and laughed until I was gasping for breath, dabbing my eyes with my sleeves. So, yes, it has been surprisingly therapeutic.

But, as I've explored my own journey, I've also looked at the role other people have played in my life. I've gained insight and an understanding and hopefully even found some compassion, although I still feel strongly that we all need to take responsibility for our lives and actions.

I still believe that denial is unhelpful.

I've learnt I do not forgive easily. But I accept.

I've also often been asked why I don't mention his name. And the reason is simple. This is not his story. It is mine.

Besides, he's not entitled to the privilege. He doesn't deserve the honour in my life. He could have been anyone – the *who* behind the *he* has become irrelevant.

Although, admittedly, there have been times when I wrote about him that I wished he'd never been. When I relived some of the scenes and as they came alive, there were many occasions when I was crippled by his presence, terrified of him all over again. But mostly I was angry, or sad. I hope that over the years he has been able to look inward and make some positive changes, but I'm not convinced that could ever happen as he has never felt the need to apologise or reach out to me to make any amends.

And as I sit in my office typing these last words, I look up and stare out of my window to the wide landscape that stretches beyond. I have spent the last year looking down, typing furiously, but today I look up and I see Table Mountain before me. She is standing proud and resolute. I watch as her cloud lifts lightly, then scatters and I look out over her edges in wonder.

Acknowledgements

I remember my very last day of school as I walked with my friends around the formal gardens, our arms linked tight as we moved together with youthful abandon, our green school dresses grown too short. We strolled around and around, the jacaranda trees dropping their purple blooms on us like confetti as each of us shared our dreams and hopes for the future. I was going to be a TV presenter, a fashion designer, and one day I'd write a book. My life in fashion was short-lived, after circumstances with my father and what was happening in my life at the time brought that part of my dream to an end. It was fortuitous, though, as I have loved my career as a TV and radio presenter and, of course, I have learnt enormously from this experience of writing a book. I might even write another one. But thank you, Dianne Blount, Carol Maclennan, Joy Ackerman and Robyn Holmes for being a part of my dreams.

I hadn't been living in Cape Town very long when I was invited to join a running group. They had been running together for many years and weren't really open to expanding and bringing in anyone new, but somehow my friend Ruth Scholtz convinced them to include me. They were a small group of six. Every Tuesday I'd join them as they took to Newlands forest and ran the upper and lower contours, scrambled over rocks, searched for porcupine quills, and stopped to take photos. It was only after many months of running together that I found out who Mike was. Mike Behr was the journalist who'd written that beautiful, sensitive, fateful *Fair Lady* article that had drawn my abuser to me. Mike had interviewed me telephonically at the time, so I had had no idea of what he looked like. He is very tall.

It then transpired that petite, lovely Elizabeth – also in the running group – was the sister of that wonderful woman, the ex-girlfriend, Cathy, who so bravely came out in my defence at the very end, after my trial.

What are the chances?

Somehow the beginning and the end were running on either side of me. It seemed unbelievable and I took it as another sign that now was the time to sit down and remember and finally tell my story. So thank you, Mike and Elizabeth, and of course thank you, Cathy, for being so terribly brave and being the ending to my book.

Over the years there have been many others by my side.

Charlene Smith, Miranda Friedman, Katherine Bester and my mother, Liza, thank you for giving up all those days over a two-and-a-half-year period to sit on those hard benches, never wavering in your support.

Thank you to Karen de Waal for thirty years of friendship, for never missing a day in court and for always believing in me.

To Estie Morgan, thank you for being my staunchest supporter and dear friend.

Thank you to Sue Grant-Marshall for being my court support, my daughter's godmother and my fascinating wordsmith friend.

Sandra Maat and Sheryl Michelow, thank you for being the best. We all knew the system was always going to be against us. But we are enough.

Amy Taylor, thanks for being my reader, and for your youthful, reassuring enthusiasm.

Sam Kalis, thanks for listening as I plotted and mulled out loud each chapter while our feet pounded the hills of Constantia.

Ashleigh Hamilton-Moore, for holding the light aloft despite your own trying circumstances – thanks for the coffees, insight, the laughs and your new-old friendship.

To my husband, Arnaud, I know you're not a reader and will never open this book, but thank you for giving me the time and space to write it.

To my Going family, thank you for allowing me to tell my story; for your understanding and support. I love you all, Dave, Fi, Roy and Marg.

To my cousin Nikki Going for holding me up when I was having fevered second thoughts and for taking my words so calmly in your gentle hands, for reassuring me, and for coming up with the elusive title.

Thank you to Sean Fraser for editing, for sifting my words through your brilliant, brilliant mind.

Then, lastly, there was only one person in this harsh but beautiful world that I wanted holding my life story in her hands and it was Melinda Ferguson. Melinda, thank you for believing in me and carrying me through the unknown.

It turns out that Melinda shares her birthday with my father.

What are the chances?

Unbelievable.

Thank you for reading my story.